T0103916

MERRILL PHILLIPS

Trafford rev. 03/11/2014

 www.trafford.com

North America & international
toll-free: 1 888 232 4444 (USA & Canada)
fax: 812 355 4082

BE WISE AND CHOOSE
WELL WHAT YOU WANT
TO INFLUENCE YOUR
LIFE

MERRILL PHILLIPS

CONTENTS

FROM SINNER TO SAINT

Luke 15:7
I say to you that likewise there will be more joy in heaven over one sinner who repents than over ninety-nine just persons who need no repentance.

Although I know not the sequence that takes place when one is changed from a sinner to a saint, but I do know that it can and does happen.

I am proof that God loves us and if we submit to His ways or express the desire to be more like Him that He will complete the process of us becoming a saint.

This desire to change must come from the heart and be foremost in our thoughts for the betterment of our lives, the desire to cast off the old and put on the new.

He will change our lives completely, from acquiring new friends to even changing our residency.

In my case, God allowed me to witness his "Light", (the same light Saul saw on the road to Damascus) and from that moment on my whole life changed.

God lifted me out of the addiction to alcohol and healed my kidneys that were failing because of alcohol abuse.

In nineteen eighty-two I closed a prosperous plumbing business, sold our property in New Hampshire and moved to Saint Louis, Mo. where my daughter lived at the time.

For the most of three years, while in St. Louis I worked for a construction company building new homes. I became his lead man in specialty trades.

From there we moved to Phoenix, Arizona where I worked as a handyman. While in Phoenix, the Lord called me to write for him. Within six months, I began to write and have been writing ever since.

After the death of our granddaughter who lived in Saint Louis we moved to Farina, Illinois where I operated an apple orchard.

After three seasons of running an apple orchard, the Lord told me one day while storing firewood for the coming winter "You will not be here to burn any of this wood."

True to his word within two months, the owner of the orchard announced that he was selling the orchard and we would have to be out by the first of the year.

From there we moved to Canton, Mississippi. While there, I worked for the First Baptist Church as their janitor. When I reached their retirement age of sixty five I was cut loose.

We were attracted to Canton because two of my wife's children lived in that general area. The job as janitor allowed me quite a bit of spare time and during this time, I wrote and shared my writings with the clientele of my wife's beauty shop.

From Canton, we moved to Barton, Mississippi, where we reside to this day. We eventually joined the Barton Methodist Church where we became a member of a close-knit family of believers.

While in Barton, I worked for Argo Construction Co. who builds highways and develops subdivisions. I worked in their maintenance division and although I am now seventy-six years of age, I still work four ten hour days per week.

Through all of these changes of residencies and having to find work, I have never once gone without a steady paycheck. God has provided work for me everywhere we have lived. Although anxious about work at times, I have never been without a job.

I can testify that God is true to his word and will never leave us or forsake us. If He were to tell me now that I should move to a new location I would not hesitate to do so, for I know in advance that He will supply all of my needs.

Submitting to whatever God wants of me has been both a joy and very fulfilling. I have gained a peace and confidence in the one who created me that can only be gained through obedience to ones calling.

Though I will never have an abundance of earthly goods, I know that I will never go without.

I thought that God had given me a gift beyond my abilities. Guess what? I was wrong, for along with the gift of writing God has given me the ability to express what he wants me to convey. I do not always think that I do a good job, but that I will leave up to those who read my offerings and will humbly accept their thoughts. Be they good or bad.

Through this whole portion of my life, I have grown more spiritually and have come to love God, Jesus Christ, and the Holy Ghost as to where they are foremost in my life.

Why I was given the gift of writing I may never know, but I do know that it has allowed me to express myself and thoughts in ways I before never thought possible. It is a humbling way of life, but I enjoy it.

Writing can also be a lonesome way of life, for it demands much time and it seems as though I do not have enough time to devote to it as I should.

I declare that Jesus Christ is the Master of my life and whatever He calls me to do I will do it to the best of my ability, no matter where it might lead. This life is an adventure so why not follow Jesus and enjoy what time we do have here on earth.

The day fast approaches when I will hear Jesus call my name and it will be time for me to leave this world and make my final journey to my Savior's side.

I have at least one more move to make and one more place to live and according to God's word; I will spend eternity in the presence of Jesus Christ as one of his followers.

GIFTS

2 Timothy 1:6
Therefore I remind you to stir up the gift of God which
is in you through the laying on of my hands.

God sits on his throne, eyes so bright, countenance so fair, with nothing but love in His heart for you and me.

Beside Him his angels stand, ready to obey His every command, shinning so bright in God's holy light.

A light so bright that it lights up the whole of heaven and reveals the path that man should trod.

A path that chastens the seeking heart and cleanses the soul as through the trials of life man goes.

A fitting place for man to be before the throne of God, asking God to heal his hurting soul.

It is with love that God touches the heart of man and leads him back to his fold.

With His mighty hand, God gives gifts to man, a different gift for everyone, a task for man to unfold.

The gift that God cast my way was one of writing for Him, completely unprepared and ill equipped I ventured to fulfill my calling.

Slowly at first with great trepidation, I set about putting words together in such a fashion as to create prose that would be helpful to whosoever might read.

It is not my place to judge my own works, nor do I intend to presume that I am an educated author.

I am but a wayward child that God took by the hand and declared, "Follow me". So, I merely follow that which the Lord God instructs me to do.

At times, I interject too much "I" and He reprimands me and tells me to leave "I" where it had ought to be.

So, it is and has been a time to reflect on and portray the truths of God by waiting upon the Lord to put into my heart that which He wants me to say.

It is with great humility that I submit unto you offerings that only you can judge whether or not they help you in your daily walk with God.

God is the giver of life and the giver of gifts and he never asks anything that He will not provide whatever is needed to fulfill his gifts.

God works in His own way and His own time and His timing is perfect, and once we accept that we are of value to Him in what He has called us to do.

If per chance, I overrun my bounds God cuts the flow of words off until such time as I put self aside and wait on Him to finish what He wants me to portray.

It is a matter of obedience to fulfill the gifts that God bestows upon those who He chooses to fulfill His will among men.

It is not my place to choose how or where my gift will be used, it is however, my place to fulfill God's command and to let Him bring my offerings to light in His time and place.

So it is with great pleasure and obedience that I keep on writing until the day God calls me home.

I need not know why God chose me to write. One day it will all become clear and that is all that I need to know.

ALL KNOWING GOD

Jeremiah 31:33
But this is the covenant that I will make with the house of Israel after those days, says the lord; I will put my laws in their minds, and write it in their hearts; and I will be their God and they shall be My people.

As we bury our dead, their souls have already returned to God and He has administered His judgment and assigned them to their proper place of abode.

God knew us before we were born and unto Him we return upon the death of the flesh.

Before death, we have already made our decision where we will spend eternity. God just makes that decision final. It is we ourselves, not God who condemns us to hell or allows us to abide in heaven; we do it by our own actions while we still have breath in our bodies.

Why should we blame God for the decisions that we make in regards as to where we will spend eternity. We are corruptible and go astray, God is perfect and cannot look upon evil. God see right through the evil that we proclaim good and try to pass it off as good.

God knows our heart and judges us by what is in our heart, it is just that simple, we either exalt ourselves or we condemn ourselves by which we allow to enter our heart.

God gives us every possible chance to spend eternity with him, it is we who accept that opportunity or reject it.

God even sent his only Son, Jesus Christ to help us make the right decision. Many have rejected Jesus Christ in their hearts and by doing so they condemn themselves to hell, not God.

Those who have accepted Jesus Christ in their hearts and live by His commandments have also sealed their destination after death, only in this case they shall spend eternity with their creator, God.

God's ways are so simple that even a sinner like myself can discern the difference from good and evil, thus will I like all who believe will spend eternity with God.

Closing ones heart to God is the same thing as slamming the door in God's face and not allowing His love to have a positive influence in our lives.

An open heart on the other hand welcomes God and His influence in their lives and seeks the positive influence it will have on their lives.

The flesh shall be discarded after death and only the soul shall survive to spend eternity wherever God decrees.

The soul can be smothered by the desires of the flesh and yet it is the soul that has to influence the flesh for good in order to spend eternity with God.

We are like two enmities in one, the flesh and the soul come together as one and yet each one has its own identity, both must reconcile as one in order to live in harmony with God.

There are many influences in this life and they are categorized into two distinct categories, one being good and the other being evil.

One must accept or reject each category on its own merits and it comes down to one thing and one thing only. Either we accept God, Jesus Christ, and the Holy Spirit as the way that we want to follow or we accept Satan and his ways as our guide in life, we cannot follow both.

We are truly involved in a spiritual battle where evil (Satan) is trying to dominate over good (God) and we (Your soul and mine) is the prize.

In the final analysis God shall prevail, so it behooves us to follow Jesus Christ rather than Satan, Satan cares less, all he is in interested in is to destroy all of God's children that he can, he so hates God for not sharing his throne with him that he revolted against God and was thrown out of heaven

ALWAYS THERE

Psalm 100:4
Enter into His gates with thanksgiving, and into his courts with praise. Be thankful to him, and bless his name.

Almighty God as the hours turn into days, days into weeks, weeks into months and months into years, shelter us from the sins of the flesh.

Guide and direct us as we go about our daily tasks and comfort us as we go through the trials of life, for they are many and diversified.

Heavenly Father we thank Thee for all of the blessings that you bestow upon each and every day.

We are unworthy of Your love and yet you shower it upon us in abundance, we regret the times that we fail to thank you.

Father God, cool the fevered brow, comfort the sick and the dying, that all hearts be opened to Your love.

Even in death, You are with us and we ask that You remove its sting.

O Lord You have to be a gracious God, because You loved us enough to send Your Son, Jesus Christ, to be an acceptable sacrifice for our sins.

When He died upon that cross at Calvary, He fulfilled the scriptures and opened the door to eternal life for all who have and will accept Him as Your loving Son.

O God You are always there whenever we are in need, just by coming to You in prayer You listen and then fulfill Your will in our lives as is best for us.

You being the creator of all that there is, we beseech You to guide and comfort us as we journey through this life that You have so graciously given unto us.

This world is truly a haven in space where we can work out our salvation and yet it is only a speck in the vastness of your creation.

Whereupon leaving this haven the tares shall be separated from the wheat and each shall go their appointed way.

For this and all that, You do on our behalf every day we give thanks.

AMAZING "LIGHT"

Ephesians 5:8
For you were once darkness, but now you are light in
the Lord. Walk as children of light.

The "Light" of God is an amazing "Light", it is many
hundreds times as bright as the sun.

Human eyes cannot look upon God's "Light" without being
destroyed in the process. Only our spiritual eyes can gaze upon His
"Light" and survive.

Whoever has had the privilege of seeing this "Light" is changed
forever, in the twinkling of an eye God has changed the lives
of many.

All who see this "Light" will never forget what it has done for
them; many have closed businesses, changed jobs, refrained from
the sins that were dominating their lives, turned to God and lived
more productive lives.

They have sort out churches where they make new friends and
contribute to the growth of God's kingdom here on earth.

No one is ever the same after witnessing the "Light" of God,
the change is always for the better.

Second Corinthians 4:6 KJV says it best. For God who
commanded the light to shine out of darkness hath shined in our
hearts, to give the light of knowledge of the glory of God in the
face of Jesus Christ.

AN EXAMPLE FOR ALL

Isaiah 30:21
Your ears shall hear a word behind you, saying, "This is the way, walk in it." Whenever you turn to the right hand or whenever you turn to the left.

Our Lord Jesus Christ sowed the seeds of Christianity wherever He went.

He opened His heart and healed the sick and the lame, the lepers were cleansed by just His word, and the seas obeyed His commands.

Whosoever receives the word and nourishes it in their heart will turned from their sinful ways and be saved.

The un-righteous go their own way and in the end, they will pay the price for ignoring what Jesus has to say.

Jesus advocated that all should seek forgiveness and that all should forgive trespasses against them in order to live as He proclaimed.

Jesus left His heavenly home so that you and I might be saved through his crucifixion and resurrection, what a great plan.

He knew before He came to earth that He would be the sacrifice for the sins of man and yet He came so that all who live in this world might be saved.

Jesus was and still is in complete control of all things here on earth, nothing escapes his attention, great or small.

Where else can we go to receive forgiveness of our sins and rise above them unharmed?

Jesus Christ holds the answers to all of our problems and will gladly give us the answers that we need if only we would call upon Him whenever we are in need.

Bless us Lord Jesus as we pray day by day for a better life and the assurance that you will go before us and pave the way.

It is Jesus, not we ourselves who can free us from the bondage of sin, for we cannot see beyond the pleasures of the sins that are leading us down the road to hell.

Jesus is always ready to set us free, it is we who refuse to give up the pleasures of the flesh and allow His will of to be done in our lives.

Humbleness and the acknowledgment that Jesus Christ is the answer to all of our problems is hard for us to accept and it is hard for us to give up self so that Jesus can become part of our life.

How long will it take us to humble ourselves before the throne of Jesus and seek His will in all that we do?

Without the example that Jesus Christ set we would still be wandering in the darkness of sin, never knowing the freedom that He offers all who accept Him as their Lord and Savior.

ARE YOU READY TO MEET JESES

Hebrews 12:6
For whom the Lord loves He chastens, and scourges every son whom He receives.

If you should meet Jesus Christ face to face today are you ready to say, "I love you Jesus. Take my hand and lead the way."

Did you pray last night for Jesus to take your fears away?

Did you thank Him for taking your place on the cross at Calvary and freeing you from the bondage of sin?

Are you grateful enough to go forth and spread his word?

Have you bent your knees before His throne and asked Him to forgive you of your sins?

What if Jesus said "I know thee not", would you curse Him and be lost, or would you throw yourself at His feet and beg Him for mercy?

What if you were to die today would your soul go to heaven or end up in hell?

There is a way to avoid having to answer these questions. It is simple and easy to do.

Go to Jesus in prayer and ask Him to come into your life, ask Him to forgive you of your sins.

Accept Jesus Christ as Lord and Savior of your life. Let Him know that you love Him by obeying His commandments.

Listen and do whatever He asks you to do. He will not burden you with anything that you are not capable of doing.

He will provide you with everything that you will need to do it, no matter what it is.

One day you will look back and say, "Why didn't I turn to Jesus sooner. I have never felt this fulfilled before."

Following Jesus will change your life and your life habits for the better. No longer will you go to sleep at night and have to worry where your soul will go when it comes your time to leave this earth.

Sins that you once indulged in and enjoyed will no longer rule your life, you will be free of the consequences of your repented sins and will have a sense of peace that you had never known before.

You will have contentment in your life, no matter whether you are rich, poor, or a beggar on the street.

You will know that you know you will spend eternity with Jesus Christ and not have to second-guess when someone asks you if Jesus Christ is the center of your life.

It will be the greatest feeling that you will ever have when you are able to answer the question "Do you know Jesus Christ as Lord of your life?" in a positive manner.

Make that change today, tomorrow may be too late. Jesus is waiting for you to come before Him in humbleness and ask Him to change your life.

ASSURANCE

Hebrews 6:11
And we desire that each one of you show the same
diligence to the full assurance of hope until the end.

Being saved and assured of going to heaven is as simple as accepting Jesus Christ as being the Son of God.

Not just verbally saying it, but believing that it is true in your heart.

The tongue says what the brain tells it to say, but from the heart comes what the soul accepts as the truth.

Good deeds are wonderful and we should do more of them, but good deeds by themselves will not open the door to heaven.

Good works come as the results of believing that Jesus Christ is the Son of God, not a means by which someone can be saved and enter heaven.

We complicate things by not believing that simplicity is the mainstay of being saved, for God's ways are simple and straightforward.

Satan will do all that he can to confuse the issue of being saved by presenting many different avenues by which one may be saved and it is up to the believer to search the Bible to satisfy themselves that he or she has chosen the right path.

As Jesus has told us, we cannot come to the Father but by through Him, so must we believe and act accordingly.

By believing in Jesus as the key to heaven, we open the door to all kinds of blessings and all kinds of help when we are in need.

Jesus blesses us every day as long as we hold Him as the Lord and Master of our lives, it is with such assurance that we become a child of God.

God never said do this and that and you will be saved, he said believe in my Son and such believers will be rewarded the keys to heaven.

In good times and in bad hold on to the truths according to the Bible and this life and its problems will not overwhelm you.

This life is a place where one prepares him or herself for the life that comes after the grave, either with Jesus as the Son of God or with Satan in the lake of fire, separated from God for eternity.

To have that blessed assurance of spending eternity with Jesus Christ is as simple as accepting Him as the one and only Son of God.

Turn from the ways of this world and hold to your God given right to become a child of God and wonder not where you will spend eternity.

AWAKENING

Psalm 17:15
As for me, I will see your face in righteousness; I shall
be satisfied when I awake in Your likeness.

From the depth of winter to the warmth of spring, the
flowers sleep and then awaken to begin life anew.

We as Christians can become like the flowers during the cold
of winter, we fall asleep and are tempted to go back to our old ways.

The ways of the flesh where we disregard the small still voice
within us that tries to awaken our souls and return to following Christ.

Many never do return to Christ in the way that they once did,
because the ways of the flesh become too tempting to resist.

Accumulated wealth, partying, travel, all of these please the
flesh and we embellish the ways of the flesh more than the ways
of God.

These temptations become too enjoyable to think about giving
them up, they satisfy the lusts of the flesh and we might say, "One
day I will return to and live the way that Christ would want me to
live, but for now I think I will enjoy myself while I have the chance".

The back sliders might just do as they say and one-day return to
the ways of the Lord, but what if while they were enjoying the lust
of the flesh they should die. What then?

Would they give up their rightful place in heaven? Would God
say, "Sorry you don't measure up." Would they be cast into outer
darkness?

These and many more questions arise as to where they will
spend eternity. Will God forgive without repentance? Will He turn
his head and allow them to live with him for eternity?

There is nowhere in the Bible that allows such un-repented sins
to go unnoticed or be forgotten without repentance.

Merrill Phillips

Is once saved always saved? This in itself is a question that is debated even among the greatest of scholars. Can we in fact sin and get away with it?

There is only one time when we will know the answers to all of these questions and that is when we die and meet God and stand before His judgment seat.

Do you want to wait to that time and have no chance to repent if that is what is required of you?

Once death has taken our life here on earth it is too late to repent, too late to change our ways. Would it not be prudent to change our ways before death and not have to be concerned as to whether God will allow us to dwell in heaven with him?

As for me, I am a struggling sinner striving every day to improve my chances of being allowed to spend eternity in the presence of God.

I seek his forgiveness for the sins I still commit, for no matter how hard I try I will never be able to please God in the state which I now live.

We can only try and keep trying until we reach that point where we know that even though we are still a sinner God has forgiven us our sins and we know that because of that fact we will spend eternity in His presence.

This possibility is open to all people, regardless of their status in life. God loves all of us equally, he has no favorites. It is we who hold ourselves back from fulfilling our dream of eternal bliss.

If we wait until we are perfect or even better than we are now we will never be good enough on our own to achieve the level of perfection that we think that we should before God will accept us as one of his anointed.

We can only try and never give up our dream of reaching the point where we know that we will spend eternity with God.

We are now like the flowers of winter waiting for the warmth of spring to bring us back to life and blossom in the presence of God when we leave our earthly bodies behind and venture forth into a new life, one in the presence of God, Himself.

WHY BAD THINGS HAPPEN TO GOOD PEOPLE

Romans 12:21
Do not be overcome by evil, but overcome evil with good.

1— To test our faith
2— To wean us from this world.
3— To increase our faith.
4— To show us where our priorities are.
5— To reveal what we love the most.
6— To teach us obedience.
7— Bad things happen to good people because we live in a sin filled world.
8— For God to reveal his compassion towards us.
9— To help develop our spiritual growth.
10—To enable us to help others through their trials.

BAPTISM

Ephesians 4:5-6
One Lord, one faith, one baptism; one God and Father
of all, who is above all, and through all, and in you all.

Baptism is an outward sign of our inner love for the one who created us.

A promise to God that we will strive to live a Christ like life and live by the ten commandments and hold them holy, with a willing heart to raise our children to love God and put Him first in their lives.

To pass on love to our fellowman by demonstration and deed.

Baptism is not a prerequisite to entering heaven upon the death of our body.

The only prerequisite to entering heaven is that we accept Jesus Christ as the only Son of God and believe in His doctrine.

Baptism cannot wash our sins away, but it can prepare us to accept Jesus on His terms, not our own.

Baptism can prepare the heart for the coming of Jesus Christ in our lives.

Baptism is but one of many steps that we can take to show that we take God the Father, God the Son, and God the Holy Ghost, seriously.

BE STILL

Psalm 46:10
Be still and know that I am God; I will be exalted
among the nations, I will be exalted in the earth!

Be still my soul and allow the voice of the Holy Spirit to
guide you.

Listen and you shall hear above the voice of sin what God has
in store for you.

He will blot out your transgressions and set you free if you will
but follow His ways.

Where else can one find such love, no, not in all of the universe
is there a love like God's love.

All doctrines outside of God's doctrines are false and when
tested against the scriptures will be found wanting.

O my soul endeavor to see beyond self, fall on your knees
before the throne of God and praise His Holy name.

God will uplift you and give you the strength to endure the
trials of life.

God will remove all fear and put your heart at rest when death
knocks at your door.

For in God there is no death or fear, both are of this world and
one day this world will cease to be.

Even time itself will come to an end, then will God's elect
enjoy the love that passes all understanding.

One day Jesus shall return and take His own onto Himself and
thus fulfill the prophecies of old.

Be still my soul, listen for His voice, for the day fast approaches
when these words shall be fulfilled.

BE VIGILANT

1 Peter 5:8
Be sober, be vigilant, because your adversary the devil walks about like a roaring lion, seeking whom he may devour.

The longer one studies the Bible and the more one learns about Jesus Christ and His role in the lives of believers, the more one becomes to realize that this world is under the influence of Satan.

Satan is the great deceiver and it is the duty of all Christians to be vigilant and on guard against his efforts to draw them away from Jesus.

Satan has no special interest in anyone, except to get as many as possible to fall prey to his deceitful ways, and once we have done so he loses interest in us and goes on to his next victim.

Satan can appear as a bright and morning star, but behind this facade he is like a roaring lion, ready to devour any and all who are weak and follow his deceitful temptations.

He is as a wolf is sheep's clothing, like a chameleon that changes his spots to suit himself and his agenda.

Once one has succumbed to Satan's deceitful ways they cannot on their own break the strings that Satan has bound them with.

The only effective way to break the strings that Satan binds one with is to reach deep inside of themselves and put on the whole armor plate of God and allow God to do their battle for them.

Even as one turns to God for help Satan will do his best to keep them from accepting the help that God is showering them with, for it is truly a spiritual battle between good and evil that one wages every day of their lives.

Satan has no defense against the truths of God and in reality, he is powerless against God, God has given Satan permission to tempt man and that is all.

As man grows in the knowledge of God, he comes to realize that Satan only has the power of temptation and not the power to force him to do anything against his will; through this realization, man is able to withstand the temptations of Satan.

Even though one may fall prey to the temptations of Satan they do have within themselves the ability to overcome those temptations through coming before the throne of God and repenting of their sins.

God being the loving God that He is is willing to forgive the repentant heart and restore us as a sheep of His pasture, free from the sins that once bound us and kept us from doing what was right.

As the temptations of Satan can keep us from our Saviors side, so can a repentant heart be vigilant and restore us as a follower of Jesus Christ.

One day man will be free from the temptations of Satan through the death of the flesh. That is when man will find out just how good of a job he did here on earth to withstand the temptations of Satan, and this is when he will be rewarded for his efforts to either resist Satan or fall prey to his evil ways.

BE WISE

Ephesians 5:15
See then that you walk circumspectly, not as fools but
as wise, redeeming the time, because the days are evil.

Though we may have close friends and family, every one walks their own pathway of life and must make their own decisions as to how they live their life.

We as individuals are responsible for our own decisions even though influenced by others.

God makes no distinction between a husband or wife or family members, He treats them all the same and rewards them according to their acceptance of His Son, Jesus Christ.

To accept Jesus Christ, as God's Son is the most important decision that anyone will ever make in his or her life, for Christ is the center of Christian living.

One cannot love God and do evil deeds, for the two are worlds apart. One can and will be tempted to go astray, even Christians are tempted, but when they are, they know that they can call upon God to help them to overcome temptations.

God is a loving God and has laid out the pathway that all should follow and yet He has given us free choice to walk whichever pathway we choose to follow.

There being only two pathways for man to follow. One is the pathway that leads to heaven and the other pathway leads to hell, so be wise as to which one you choose to follow.

The straight and narrow pathway is the harder one to follow, but in the end, it leads to heaven and eternal life with our Lord and Master, Jesus Christ.

The other pathway is easy to follow, for it is wide and has many enticing and exciting things to please the flesh, but at the end of this pathway is hell, where one will be tormented for eternity, separated from God forever.

Once one has passed through the door of death it is too late to change pathways, you made your final decision before death occurred and God will respect your decision and assign you your final destination.

No one is perfect and never will be as long as they live, for we live in a sin-filled world under the influence of Satan. This life consist of a spiritual battle between good and evil and Satan is the prince of this world, but at the same time Satan himself is under the control of God and has limited powers.

Though Satan has the power of temptation, he can in no way force us to obey his temptations, no matter how strong they might be. With God's help, we can overcome any temptation that Satan tempts us with.

As a craftsman knows the difference between the different woods that he uses in his profession, so does God know the difference between a good heart and an evil one, for our deeds give us away. Good will follow good and evil will follow evil.

BEACON UNTO MY SOUL

Psalm 27:1
The Lord is my light and my salvation; whom shall I fear? The Lord is the strength of my life; of whom shall I be afraid?

I commend my soul unto Thee O Lord; strip me of my earthly ties, for I belong to Thee.

Lest I lose courage and return to my old ways, and lose my life by the hand of Satan.

Strip me of my earthly ties O Lord before the darkness of death overtakes me.

In my youth, I squandered my time on the things of the flesh.

As old age approached, I began life anew, I was born again, I had a new life with a new beginning.

Freed from the ties of the past I gained favor with you O Lord, and left the treasures of earth second in line.

With your forgiving love O Lord, I commend my soul unto You, and will rest in Your arms for eternity.

Blessed be Thy name Holy Father, it stands as a beacon unto my soul, a beacon of light and hope.

Strip me of my earthly ties Father God, creator of all; strip me bare and Yours I will be for eternity.

The flesh is weak and Thou art strong, Thou art the answer to my prayers.

Whether my life is short or long I pray that, You will strip me of my earthly ties and draw me closer to Thee.

You are a beacon unto my soul, a beacon by which I can steer my ship of life by through the shoals of sin.

A beacon who's Light never grows dim, it stands before the whole world and draws all righteous souls unto God, the one who created everything from the beginning unto the end.

OUR EYES SHALL BEHOLD THE GLORY OF GOD

John 1:14
And the word became flesh and dwelt among us, and
we beheld His glory, the glory as of the only begotten
of the Father, full of grace and truth.

When our eyes begin to grow dim and the light begins to
fade, we can face our mortality unafraid.

By accepting Jesus Christ as our Savior, we take victory from
the grave and the sting out of death.

We no longer hold any fear of dying; we just close our eyes and
leave this world in peace.

Our future is bright when in Jesus Christ we believe; He took
our sins upon Himself and overcame them at Calvary.

Our journey from here to eternity is sure and swift; we pass
through the heavens in the twinkling of an eye and embrace Jesus
on the other side.

The journey of death began the day that we were born and
those who live by God's commands death to life eternal holds no
concern.

Jesus is the "Light" of this world and He stands at the gate to
heaven waiting for his sheep to take their place in His fold.

Once in heaven we will eat of the fruit of the tree of life and
forever be with the Lord.

Every promise Jesus ever made will be fulfilled before our eyes
and the fears of the flesh will never more affect our lives.

Only those who reject Jesus before they die will be turned aside
when the shadow of death covers their eyes.

They made their decision to follow other gods long before they died and as a result, God knew them not on the other side.

Hold the hand of Jesus and He will walk before you and bestow upon you the gift of life eternal when you die.

BELIEVE IN JESUS

Romans 10:9
That if you confess with your mouth the Lord Jesus and believe in your heart that God has raised Him from the dead, you will be saved.

Peace shall reign for those who forsake the ways of the flesh and follow Jesus wherever He may lead.

To forsake Jesus is to lose ones live and die at the hands of sin, to live is to accept Jesus and upon the death of the flesh return to Jesus and live with Him for eternity.

Satan can give pleasure to the flesh while it is still day, but as day fades into night so shall the followers of Satan fade into obscurity.

Darkness (sin) cannot comprehend the Light, nor can it hide the Light (Jesus) from those who seek the "Light".

Wherever the "Light" of Jesus shines, the darkness of Satan flees and no more will it influence the children of "Light".

This is a promise of God that the darkness of Satan can be replaced by the "Light" of Jesus.

Seek the treasures of Jesus and store them in your heart and they in turn will drive Satan from your door.

As the sun replaces the darkness of the night at the break of day, so shall the "Light" of Jesus displace the wickedness of Satan when we accept Jesus as our Savior and Lord of our lives.

It is Jesus working through us that helps others to believe, not us working through Jesus, we are a tool for good in the hands of Jesus.

The day approaches when Satan will have no more influence over our lives, but until that day hold fast to the truths of Jesus as set forth in the Bible and your walk through this life will be more pleasurable.

Jesus fought the final battle against evil (Satan) while He hung on the cross at Calvary and triumphed over him, thus setting you and me free from the bondage of sin.

Jesus gave His life for us because He loves us and wants you and me to spend eternity with Him in a world where there will never again be any evil or sin or disease to tempt us.

Just a simple step of faith can be the most rewarding act that you or I will ever take, believing in Jesus has rewards beyond our comprehension, now is the day to make that decision.

BELIEVE AND TRUST IN JESUS

Proverbs 3:5-6
Trust in the Lord with all of your heart, and lean not on your own understanding; in all your ways acknowledge Him, and he shall direct your paths.

Join those who believe that Jesus Christ is Lord of lords and King of kings and your life will never be the same.

From the moment, you believe your heart will be full of joy and you will proclaim that Jesus Christ is the Captain of your life and keeper of your soul.

Your days will be brighter, and when in need you will go to your knees and consult the new Master of your life, from there He will lead.

Your eyes will sparkle every time you hear His name and before long you will be able to see beyond the clouds of sin that once blinded you.

The Light of Jesus will light up your life and to your neighbor you will proclaim, "Jesus has changed me from a sinner to a Saint and if you would, join me, please".

By the way you change and live will be a sure sign that you will not change your mind or follow the temptations that once dominated your life.

Forgiveness of sin is yours now that you have forgiven those who trespassed against you when in the secular world you spent all of your time.

All it takes is a moment of time to turn from your sins and seek the one who set you free when on the cross He hung at Calvary.

Merrill Phillips

To Jesus we owe it all, to Him we pray when Satan tempts us to go astray and indulge in sin that could keep us from our Savior's side.

Believe in Jesus and your life will change in the wink of an eye, praising Him for the love that He shows for you and me, leaving the secular world behind.

BEYOND TOMORROW

Matthew 6:34
Therefore do not worry about tomorrow, for tomorrow
will worry about its own things. Sufficient for the day
is its own trouble.

There is a day a-coming beyond tomorrow that has no end or any sorrow.

Lord Jesus has it ready for those who believe that He is who He claims to be.

There is no sun by day, nor moon by night, for Jesus is it's Light.

The flowers, trees, and grasses that grow along the way will dazzle the eyes, their beauty will never fade away.

The streams run cool and deep, from the throne of God they flow and run out of sight.

Their waters are for the healing of the nations, their banks they will never overflow.

Unlike the floods of Egypt, their waters bring only joy and delight.

There are no wild beasts to cause any fright, just those who graze upon the sweet grasses and rest each night.

There is a day beyond tomorrow that has no end or any sorrow.

A rainbow forms the gate that leads to the river Jordan that only the pure in heart can navigate.

The great Shepherd is there waiting for His sheep to cross the river Jordan and leave behind all who are contrite and full of fright.

Only a chosen few who are pure in heart and full of God's "Light" will be allowed to enter this new day beyond tomorrow that has no end or any sorrow.

BOOK OF BOOKS

Revelation 20:12
And I saw the dead, small and great, standing before God, and books were opened. And another book was opened, which is the Book of Life. And the dead were judged according to their works, by the things that were written in the books.

Live by the words of the Bible and live forever in the presence of God.

The truths of the Bible can free all from any and all sin, with the exception of blasphemy against the Holy Ghost.

As the Bible tells us, Jesus laid out the path which we should walk in order to achieve eternal life.

It also tells us that without Jesus' love for us we would not be able to come to Him in our hour of need and expect to be freed from our problems.

Words of the Bible themselves will not save us; they only have an influence on our lives when we willingly take them into our hearts for the purpose of improving our lives.

We can read the Bible from cover to cover and quote scripture by heart, but if we do not take these scriptures and model our lives around them then it will be like water on a ducks back.

Modeling our lives to conform to the scriptures is a process that we have to do for ourselves; it is not something that someone else can do for us.

Others can guide us and help us by telling of their experiences with Jesus, but unless we submit ourselves to the influence of the Bible, it is like standing out in the rain and expecting to stay dry.

Those who claim that the Bible is not the inspired word of God are just looking for excuses to live their lives as they want to without anyone telling them how they should live.

This is of course the freedom that God gave to all of us, but He also said throughout the Bible that if we choose to deny Jesus Christ then Jesus will deny us before the Father.

Denying Jesus leads to separation from God for eternity, being cast into the bowls of hell where the worm never dies and there is no peace, just anguish and turmoil for eternity.

The Bible provides a way that we do not have to be separated from God, a way that we can live forever in peace and love with our Creator.

The Bible is also a history of mankind, from his creation to his final disposition, either with God or lost forever.

More than history the Bible provides a means by which we can trace the lineage of Jesus Christ from Adam to our present day.

The Bible was written many centuries ago, but it is just as applicable today as it was when it was written.

It is not like other books that are a rage for a season then cast into obscurity, the Bible is a guide unto us as long as man shall lives on earth.

It also goes beyond the life of man, it tells of the new world that is not made, where the true believers shall dwell for eternity.

I don't know about you, but as for me, I intend to live the kind of life that will allow me to dwell with God forever.

God has forgiven me of my sins and I have accepted Jesus Christ as the one and only Son of God, thus qualifying me to live with Him when this earth I leave.

How about you, are you willing to give up self and live as God would have you live so that you too can live with Him forever? The Bible provides the way.

CLOSER TO JESUS

Hebrews 12:2
Looking unto Jesus, the author and finisher of our faith, who for the joy that was set before Him endured the cross, despising the shame, and has sat down at the right hand of the throne of God.

With every trial I face I draw closer to Jesus Christ.

Who else can save me from myself, who else loves me enough to take my place on the cross at Calvary and be a sacrifice for my sins?

No one but Jesus, Jesus stood in my place as I indulged in sin and patiently waited for me to turn to Him.

Jesus' love for me turned me from a sinner to a saint, from a wandering refugee to a devoted disciple.

Jesus is the one who forgave me of my sins and hung on the cross instead of me.

His "Light" lights my path as I struggle to follow Him.

With sorrow in my heart, I bend my knees before Thy throne and pledge my life to Thee.

Use me Lord Jesus as You will to promote Your kingdom here on earth.

This world will one day be no more, but Your love and forgiveness will endure throughout eternity.

Though I am not worthy to stand in Your presence, I still seek Thee in all that I do.

I pray that my offerings will display Your glory and bring a sense of peace to all of those I touch.

I seek not my glory, but point to You as Lord and Master of all who believe.

As the process of aging consumes my body, I turn to Thee and seek Thy comfort before I enter eternity.

Praying that You will accept my soul and draw me ever closer to You.

COMFORTER

Philippians 2:1-2
Therefore if there be any consolation in Christ, if any comfort of love, if any fellowship of the spirit, if any affection and mercy, fulfill my joy by being like minded, having the same love, being of one accord, of one mind.

I have been the recipient of God's love, he has blessed me far beyond my hopes and dreams.

When the storm winds of life blow I seek shelter in his love for me.

He cuddles me and protects me when Satan tries to lead me astray.

He showers me with blessings far beyond that which I deserve.

God loves me even when I am wrong, he doesn't punish me, he just nudges me and I seek his forgiveness before I do myself harm.

He has allowed me to taste the pleasures of the flesh, sweet as they were in my mouth, they were bitter in my belly.

In the end the pleasures I partook of gave me much heartache and pain.

When I turned to him and followed his plan for my life a whole new life opened up to me, one that I could not before see.

My soul rejoiced as my life changed and Jesus Christ became my Lord and Master.

As death approaches I will not fear, for my soul belongs to Jesus and all of the rest will disappear.

Now is the appointed time to seek Jesus and his grace, which is a balm to our soul.

Satan clouds the eyes of the lost so that they cannot see that which Jesus has for those who believe.

Turn to Jesus Christ before this life you leave, rejoice in his love and receive eternal life, in that you will be well pleased.

COMMUNION

2 Corinthians 13:14
The grace of the Lord Jesus Christ, and the love of
God, and the communion of the Holy Spirit be with
you all. Amen

Kneeling before the alter rail partaking of communion
brings to mind an image of bowing before the throne of God and
praising His Holy name.

Partaking of the bread and wine brings one closer to the reality
that Jesus Christ is who he claims to be and of His suffering on the
cross.

Jesus Christ freely gave his life so that you and I can have
a direct avenue of communication and personal relationship
with God.

Jesus' sacrifice was not in vain, it was however necessary in
order for us to have the hope of salvation and eternal life with God.

The cross is the symbol of hope for all of mankind, but
unfortunately there are way too few who take advantage of what
Jesus did for us.

In many cases, those who follow Jesus are looked upon by
society as being right wing fanatics who put themselves above
others.

This statement is the furthest from the truth that one can get,
for we Christians are but born again sinners who have come to
grips with our sinful past and have accepted Jesus Christ as our
Lord and Master.

This is available to one and all, without exception, for some of
the most devout Christians of today were once some of the most
evil people who ever lived.

Without Jesus Christ, none of us would have a chance of forgiveness of our sins. We owe it all to Jesus and His never-ending love for us. Seek and you will find a love beyond understanding in Jesus Christ.

Coming before the alter and partaking in communion is indeed a step in faith and appreciation of what Jesus Christ has done for us.

Partaking of communion is a way of showing our love and obedience to the call of Jesus Christ in our lives and allowing Him to set at the head of our table of life.

CREATED BY THE HAND OF GOD

Isaiah 52:7
How beautiful upon the mountains are the feet of him who brings good news, who proclaims peace, who brings glad tidings of good things, who proclaims salvation, who says to Zion, your God reigns!

I stand by the wayside gazing across a field of flowers mingled with tall grasses, waving in the gentle breezes that pass by, filling the air with the fragrance of spring.

Just beyond the field are tree-covered hills, forming a collar of green, fit to be worn by a queen.

Beyond the tree-covered hills stand majestic snow capped mountains, yet to yield to the warmth of spring.

Rugged snow capped mountains that display the strength of our creator, only the hearty dare to climb their heights and drink in the beauty that lies beyond.

Above the mountains are displayed cotton candy clouds driven by the breath of God, drifting hither and yon.

Field of flowers, hills of green, majestic mountains, sky and clouds, all created by the hand of God for of all who stop and drink in the beauty that abounds.

DEAD IN SIN

1 John 1:8
If we say that we have no sin, we deceive ourselves, and
the truth is not in us.

Forgive me O Lord my sins this day, without Thy forgiveness
surly I would be dead in sin.

Dead in our sins is surly the worst place that we could ever be,
for God will have turned his face from you and me.

He will still love us I know, but as long as we persist in sin, He
will not acknowledge us or set us free.

Oh how happy we would be if only our sins we would leave
and seek God's forgiveness on our knees.

Great will our expectations be when from our sins we leave and
turn our face towards God and behave like the children of God
that we should be.

From morning to night, everything will be all right when we
obey God and allow Him to set us free.

Oh how slothful we can be when we disobey and allow Satan
to lead us astray, and think that God cannot see.

God hears all, knows all, and sees all, from Him nothing can
be hidden, especially our sins.

Bend your knees, bow your head, turn from your sinful ways
and know that God is God, and that He will forgive the repentant
heart.

Walk in God's Light and feel it's warmth, it has healed many
a disobedient soul, rebel and die, obey and live to praise God
another day.

Now is the time to change our ways, now is the time to live
and obey, for Jesus may come today. If He does what will you say,
how will you explain your sinful ways?

If we live as we should we will not have to explain, we would not have to hide our face from His grace.

Live as though you love and care and you will not have to be concerned about tomorrow.

Bend your knees and bow your head today and proclaim your rightful place in His kingdom, don't wait, for tomorrow may never come.

DEATH

Romans 6:23
For the wages of sin is death, but the gift of God is
eternal life in Christ Jesus our Lord.

Death is part of the cycle of living and in itself is not tragic;
it is the way that one might die that can be tragic.

An example of tragic death is the way in which those aboard
the planes that hit the world trade center, pentagon, and Pa. died.

Those people were caught in a circumstance not of their
making and paid the price of being in the wrong place at the
wrong time.

Those responsible for those deaths are misguided people who
did not accept Jesus Christ and will be judged when they stand
before the judgment seat of God.

It is the way in which we die that can throw a shadow over
death, not death itself.

Those left behind (such as family and friends) find it hard to
accept the loss of loved ones.

Once on the other side of death's door those who have gone on
have no desire to return to this life, for heaven is so peaceful and
beautiful.

D— Dear departed who have completed their tour of duty here on
earth.

E— Everlasting love of God awaits the true and faithful.

A— After life is over one either spend eternity with God or the
lake of unquenchable fire.

T— The time is now to prepare for the transition from life here on
earth to life beyond the grave.

H— Happy is the person who follows Jesus Christ and dies being
at peace with himself and God.

DECISIONS

Joel 3:14
Multitudes, multitudes in the valley of decision! For the
day of the Lord is near in the valley of decision.

From believing in Jesus Christ comes the understanding that
death results in another dimension of living and death itself holds
no fear.

After death the flesh cannot leave this world, it must and will
return to the dust of the ground from which it came.

The spirit cannot remain in this world because the spirit is of
God and it shall return to Him upon the death of the flesh.

While we live, the spirit and the flesh coexist within our
bodies, one or the other will dominate, both cannot control the
actions of the body at the same time.

Either we will cling to the ways of the flesh or we will give up
the ways of the flesh and allow God to guide us in the ways that He
wants us to go.

Holding to the ways of the flesh stifles the spirit and we live
according to the desires of the flesh, which in the end leads to
spending eternity separated from God.

Our spirit is eternal, our flesh is temporal, and the pleasures of
the flesh are but for a few short years and can in no way enable us
to enter the kingdom of God.

Our spirit will endure forever, either in the presence of God or
in hell, it is here and now that we determine where we will spend
eternity.

There is only one true God and He has bestowed upon us the
freedom of choice, choose God and live, choose the ways of the
flesh and lose your place in the kingdom of God.

It is just that simple, no ifs, ands, or buts about it, and those who refuse to make a choice are lost already, and those who proclaim God and live not by His ways are also lost, for they have never accepted God as Lord and Master of their lives.

Only those who live by the word of God and accept his Son Jesus Christ as their Lord and Savior shall inherit eternal life. All could survive to spend eternity with God, but to do so they must die to the flesh and hold fast to the truths of God and exercise them in their daily lives.

There is no in between, one cannot please God while holding on to the things of the flesh, no matter what they might be.

Leaving the things of the flesh behind does not mean we have to go without the things of the flesh, what it does mean is that we are not to make the things of the flesh a god in our lives.

Things of the flesh in themselves are not deterrent in our relationship with God, it is only when we allow the things of the flesh to take the place of God that they keep us from inheriting eternal life.

Which would you rather have, the riches of this world that you can control and in so doing lose your eternal inheritance or would you rather follow God's ways and have eternal life?

This is a decision that we all have to make, to live for God or be lost to Satan.

We will choose one or the other by our thoughts, deeds, and actions, we make these choices whether we realize it or not.

Choose well my friend, for your future place of abode and my future place of abode is at stake, heaven or hell.

EARTHLY TREASURES

Matthew 6:21
For where your treasure is, there your heart will be also.

Wealth in itself is not evil; it is when we make wealth a god is where the trouble lies.

Let not the treasures of this life turn your head and put God second or third in your life.

Earthly treasures are for but a short while and in the end cannot buy even one second of life more than we were allotted.

Fame and fortune has ruined many a person and in the process, they have lost everything important.

Wealth can only buy material things, it cannot buy life eternal, it cannot buy a place in heaven, but it can however pave the road to hell.

Many who have wealth make wealth their god and live accordingly, live as though there were going to be no tomorrow.

When this life we leave we cannot take anything with us, nor can we assure ourselves a place in heaven by doing good deeds with our wealth.

God has to be the center of our lives and His ways have to be our main goal in life if we expect to inherit eternal life.

A record of our lives precede us as we step through the door of death and we will be held responsible for our actions, whether they be good or bad.

Those who have wealth do have the responsibility of using wealth responsibly, like helping their neighbor, as they would want to be helped if they were in need.

Wealth forces one to make decisions to either help their neighbor or allow wealth to become their god.

In too many cases wealth is never satisfied, it needs more and more and no matter how much wealth one accumulates it is never enough. Fear of not enough has caused many a person to hoard wealth and shut out everyone else.

In the long run all wealth and everything else belongs to God, we are but stewards of what God has given us and we will one day have to answer as to how we used what He gave us.

EVER CLOSER TO THE CROSS

Matthew 10:38
And he who does not take his cross and follow after Me
is not worthy of Me.

Jesus draws me ever closer to the cross of Calvary.

The cross upon which our Lord and Master died is a monument of His love for sinners like you and I.

Before the cross, man was headed straight to hell, for there were few who accepted the words of the Prophets as being a guide for their lives.

Man was fast approaching the same circumstances that caused God to destroy the world by the flood.

Instead, God sent His Son, Jesus Christ, as an atonement for the sins of man and by so doing God established a pathway that leads to eternal life.

Though Jesus was eventually nailed to the cross for the sins of the world He established His Church before returning to His Father above.

Many there have been who have tried to discredit and destroy the "Church", but the more they try to destroy it the bigger and more prosperous it has become.

God's Son, Jesus Christ, is the hope of all Christians, yesterday, today, and tomorrow.

Though His "Church" at times may seem to be tattered and torn, it still has the biggest influence in the world today.

Although silent at times its beacon of Light still shines and stirs the secret desires of its followers to spend eternity with its creator, Jesus Christ.

The original cross has long since been lost, but what it stands for will now and ever more be a part of Christian history.

The cross represents the struggle that Christians of the past faced and the struggle that the Christians of today face.

No matter what the bigots of tomorrow may do to discredit the cross it shall prevail as a symbol of hope to all who struggle to follow Jesus as we do today.

It is the rebellious attitude of mankind that does not want to accept the cross as a symbol of freedom the world around that makes the life of all Christians hazardous until Jesus returns one day.

It is the duty of all Christians to take up their cross and follow Jesus, even to the grave.

Though persecution for following Jesus may prevail for a time, it shall be overcome just as Jesus overcame the persecution of His day and time.

Whether or not we face trials and persecution, the cross calls us to come and take our cross and follow our Lord and Savior, Jesus Christ.

Though the cross may lead us to an early demise, we know that Jesus Christ waits for us on the other side of the cross and we like Him shall live forever, free from the influence of Satan.

EVER FORGIVING

Colossians 3:12-13
Therefore as the elect of God, holy and beloved, put on tender mercies, kindness, humility, meekness, longsuffering, bearing with one another, if anyone has a complaint against another; even as Christ forgave you, so you also must do.

Through the virgin birth, Jesus Christ came to earth to set the heart of man free.

Filled with blessings from above Jesus walked and taught throughout His created universe.

From His virgin birth to His death on the cross, Jesus set the repentant heart aglow.

The more Satan tries to stamp out the fire of freedom from sin that Jesus started so long ago the larger it grows.

Lest we forget, we all were created by Jesus and set free to do as we please.

Many there are who are blinded by the pleasures of this world and reject Jesus Christ, the one and only Son of God.

With His heart so full of love, Jesus will forgive those who turn from their sinful ways and claim Him as Lord of their lives.

The stubborn and proud who cannot see beyond their own little world face a life of torment in hell.

As humble and meek as He was, Jesus was also the creator of the universe.

Though man is fragile and made of clay, Jesus can purify him in the kiln of life to serve Him throughout eternity.

Jesus was stripped of life before the whole world, and before the whole world He arose from the grave triumphantly.

It was said by the one who nailed Him to the cross, "This man was truly the Son of God."

Just as Jesus forgave those who nailed Him to the cross, so does He even today forgive those who come before Him seeking forgiveness and the desire to live in a victorious way.

EVER ONWARD

Psalm 32:8
I will instruct you and teach you in the way that you should go; I will guide you with my eye.

He guides us ever onward towards our final goal.

In times of adversity, He extends His protective hand.

He shields us from the scorching heat of sin.

Ever onward we go, over rough ground and smooth we wind our way through the maze of life.

Ever watchful He guides us on the straight and narrow, lest we become ensnared in the web of sin.

By the bright of the moon and the heat of the day we march ever onward towards our final goal.

Facing and overcoming our past mistakes, and with the guidance of Jesus we shall not forsake.

When we reach the end of our road of life, Jesus will open the door to heaven and welcome us in.

All of our lives we have walked ever onward and worked towards this end, it will be the final triumph of our lives.

EVERLASTING PEACE

John 16:33

These things I have spoken to you, that in me you may
have peace. In the world you will have tribulation; but
be of good cheer, I have overcome the world.

Jesus is the light of my life, and in its radiance I stand.
In fair weather or foul, He holds my hand and guides me in the
path He wants me to trod.

His Light drives the darkness of death away, for in Jesus I will
never die.

At sunrise Jesus lights up the sky and paints a new picture
every day, never two the same.

Peace comes to those who allow Jesus' "Light" to shine in their
lives and put Him first in all that they do.

Even when adversity seem to overwhelm the burdened soul the
rays of heavenly peace sparks new life in the old.

Everlasting peace is of our Father from above; it is a balm for
the troubled soul.

Today, tomorrow, and forever the peace of Jesus Christ is
reinforced by the Holy Spirit in good times as well as in bad.

Peace is a gift of heavenly bliss, given to all who seek to do their
Creator's will.

May the peace of our Lord and Master, Jesus Christ, enter
your life and displace the thoughts of sin before they manifest
themselves in your life.

True peace comes in the dawning of Jesus' "Light" in our
lives, the "Light" that changes a sinner into a saint and ensures
everlasting peace.

EXPENDABLE

Ephesians 2:1
And you he made alive, you were dead in trespasses
and sins.

In the beginning God intended for man to live forever in the
fleshly body that he was given, but when sin entered his life all flesh
became expendable.

Sin contaminated the flesh and the consequences of sin is death
and after death of the flesh all that is left is the spirit.

The spirit pays for the consequences of sins of the flesh through
the second death (Separation from God for eternity).

This may paint a very bleak future for man, and so it does, for
God once destroyed all flesh through the great flood in the days
of Noah.

God caused a great flood that killed every living creature on the
face of the earth except Noah, his three sons and their wives.

They were the only ones who listened to God and did as he
commanded them, they held fast to the task of building the ark
even though the rest of the people ridiculed them and refused to
help them.

God so hates sin that if we do not repent of our sins He will
cast us from His sight, by casting us into outer darkness (hell)
where we will be tormented forever and ever.

Now is the time to repent, not after the flesh has given up the
ghost and put in the ground from which it came.

Ever since Satan was cast out of heaven for his sinful acts
against God, he has gone around like a roaring lion trying to
destroy all of God's people that he can.

Satan has only the power of temptation, but he is capable of
making temptation seem like it is the will of God, but in fact he

can be defeated by turning to God and allowing Him to fight our battles against Satan for us, if only we will ask Him to do so.

Asking by seeking God's will to be done in our lives, committing our lives to His service and opening our hearts to His loving touch.

It is not a physical battle that we fight, it is a spiritual battle, a battle that we cannot see with our eyes, and it is a battle for our souls.

God will honor all who earnestly seek Him and turn their lives over to Him so that His light can so shine through us before our fellowman that others will want what we have found.

This and this only is the way that fallen man can redeem himself so that when it becomes his time to leave this world he can enjoy what God has in store for those who love and obey Him.

It is available to all, but few there are who take God seriously enough to follow Him and enter their rightful place in God's kingdom.

Though the flesh is expendable regardless of circumstances, our spirit can live on and reap the benefits that God has in store for the faithful few who choose to live life His way, not their way.

Is it not better to forego the pleasures of the flesh and receive life eternal while it is available, rather than having to face eternity separated from God where the worm never dies and the torment never ends?

FEAR NOT

1 John 4:18
There is no fear in love; but perfect love cast out fear, because fear involves torment. But he who fears has not been made perfect in love.

Though death be all around I will fear it not, for I know that in Christ I shall live.

As I walk through this life and come to know Jesus, the fear of death flees me.

Through the scriptures, I learned that death is but the transition from carnal life to life eternal.

Though I look not forward to dying, I fear it not because Jesus walks with me.

From birth to death, we are barraged with the temptations of Satan, but those too will one day pass from view.

Jesus paid my debt for sin when on that cross He hung; I am free to be with Him when I pass to the other side.

Thank you God for the love that has set me free and one day will allow me to abide with Thee when my life is through.

FINAL VICTORY

1 Corinthians 15:57
But thanks be to God, who gave us the victory through
our Lord, Jesus Christ.

It is through death that we step into the presence of God.

While in the flesh, we can only speculate what it will be like when we enter heaven.

We are now blinded to the ways of God and cannot see beyond our sin clouded eyes.

It is only through death that we are completely released from the influence of Satan.

He (Satan) is a cleaver deceiver and makes sin enticing to the point of acceptance without question.

The day that we challenge Satan and his authority is the day that we begin our journey to true freedom.

Satan's promise of wealth and power can distracts us from our quest of living a Christ like life.

It takes a heartfelt desire to live as God intended and be strong enough to resist the easy way to wealth and fame.

Those who desire to live this type of life find it easier and easier to leave God out of their lives as they grow in self-achievement.

Meanwhile Christians who work hard to balance their lives with God as the head of their household, and keep fleshly desire where they belong find peace more rewarding than wealth.

The Christian also knows that this life is for exemplifying God here on earth amidst the struggle between good and evil.

Self-discipline is the secret to a God centered life, for within all of us is that voice that tells us right from wrong.

While in the flesh that voice can be silenced by the lusts of the eyes and thus we head down the road of self-destruction.

It takes knowledge of God to discern that which is good for us and the willingness to obey that small voice to achieve eternal life with God.

We will not all achieve the same things in life, but we can all become children of God if we so desire.

It is not God who leads us astray, it is Satan who tempts us and it is we who choose to follow Satan rather than God.

God gave us the gift of free choice and it is we who determine what we will do with our lives.

Whatever struggles we face in this life can be overcome through Jesus Christ and final victory can be ours when we acknowledge God as our creator and Jesus Christ as his only Son, our Savior.

FORGIVENESS

Ephesians 4:32
And be kind to one another, tenderhearted, forgiving one another, even as God in Christ forgave you.

Forgiveness is the duty of all how believe on Jesus Christ.

Just think of what a wonderful place this world would be if we all forgave those who trespass against us.

Just the act of forgiveness is worth more than all the gold in the world.

Forgiveness allows our bodies to be free from the stress of anger and hatred.

It opens our minds to greater things, things that we cannot see because of the clouds of sin that we live in.

Forgiveness enables our bodies to be more resistance to the ills of the flesh and to heal faster when and if we do become ill.

It is a balm to our souls, it smoothes over the scratches of discontent and mistrust.

It allows us to open our eyes and see beyond ourselves and embraces our enemies with a sense of love and hope for the future.

Forgiveness is the catalyst that binds all believers together in one common cause, the advancement of God's kingdom here on earth.

As a result we become God's representatives and are bound by His love to display the forgiveness that He (God) has shown towards us.

What greater reward could we have than to see two former enemies walk side by side in harmony down the road of life.

It is truly an inspiration to see this life through the eyes of forgiveness.

It opens a whole new world that was once clouded by distrust and sin and through forgiveness the whole world could live in harmony without the threat of discord or war.

Forgiveness is truly a gift from God, one to be treasured and given to all we meet freely.

FREE AT LAST

Galatians 5:1
Stand fast therefore in the liberty by which Christ has made us free, and do not be entangled again with a yoke of bondage.

I am now free from the bounds of the earth and walk the streets of gold.

Peace now prevails where once strife filled my life.

The sights that I now see are beyond the capabilities of earth and the imagination of man.

The voice of Jesus is music to my ears, His radiated love holds me in awe of this new world He created for saints like you and me.

I drink of the river of living waters and feast on the fruits of the tree of life.

No clouds to obscure the view of my Master's creation, colors and flowers never seen before by the likes of me.

I now live free from the temptations that Satan once threw at me, no more scales over my eyes to keep me from my Savior side.

There is a feeling that I have lived here forever, harmony beyond the ability of man.

A place that I never want to leave, singing songs of praise before the throne of God and walking on truly holy ground.

Many there are who seek to enter this place of heavenly bliss, the light of God guards the entrance to heaven and only those who have accepted His Son, Jesus Christ shall enter therein.

Free at last, never again to recall the pain of living on earth, just the present, walking and talking with Jesus Christ, and enjoying the peace and tranquility that reigns in heaven.

FREEDOM

Romans 8:2
For the law of the spirit of life in Christ Jesus has made
me free from the law of sin and death.

True love is freedom, complete freedom, not just an imitation of freedom.

Love neither binds, nor does it hinder, it leaves one with the freedom of choice.

Jesus demonstrated true love as He hung on the cross at Calvary.

Jesus gave His life so that you and I might be free from the bondage of sin.

So that we could have a choice to choose how we want to live and at the same time, Jesus set boundaries as to how we should live.

Those who accept these boundaries live a life that exemplifies the life that Jesus lived, and shall find life beyond the grave.

Every Easter we celebrate our freedom by remembering that it was Jesus who set the example of true love by giving His life so that we might have eternal life.

Jesus expressed true love without expecting anything in return and this was an example as to how we should live our lives.

Those who wish to spend eternity with Jesus will willingly follow His example by expressing true love towards their fellowman.

True love brings freedom; limited love brings heartache and strife.

GENERATION TO GENERATION

1 Peter 2:9
But you are a chosen generation, a royal priesthood,
a holy nation. His own special people, that you may
claim the praises of Him who called you out of
darkness into his marvelous light.

The healing power of Jesus Christ is free to all who earnestly seek it.

He holds back nothing from those who love Him.

He guides the fervent heart and blesses their offspring.

From generation to generation, the pure in heart have witnessed the glory of God.

Thus refuting those who say, "There is no God, He is just an illusion or a figment of their imagination."

God is holy, God is pure, God is love, and God is for now and forevermore.

As He had no beginning, He has no end; God is what life is all about.

When the trials of this life have ended, God will be there to welcome His chosen home.

The unjust shall cry for mercy and there will be no mercy.

As they showed no mercy to those who they persecuted, so shall God show them no mercy.

God chosen His elect to fulfill His will here on earth and those who answer His calling are blessed indeed.

They shall rally at the foot of the cross and carry their burdens joyfully.

Were it not for the guiding hand of God we would all be lost to the sins of this world.

Make a joyful noise unto God when He invites you to fulfill your niche in His kingdom.

He will not burden you with more than you are capable of doing.

God will supply you with all that you will need to fulfill that which He has called you to do.

God is a gracious God; His promises have and will stand the test of time.

Without God, this world and those in it would be nothing but a speck of cosmic dust.

From generation to generation, there are those whom God calls upon to promote his kingdom among the inhabitants of this world.

Jesus set the example for all who are called to follow, as He lives so shall the chosen of God live, now and forevermore.

GIFT OF LOVE

1 Corinthians 13:13
And now abide faith, hope. Love, these three; but the greatest of these is love.

One of the greatest gifts of all is the gift of love.

It cannot be bought or sold; it is free to all who open their hearts to God.

Blest are those who receive the gift of love from our Father who abides in heaven above.

God came and lived among us over two thousand years ago; He came in the flesh as Jesus Christ so that we might come to know God on our terms.

Although He was rejected and nailed to a cross He showed His love for us by dying in our place for the sins we embrace.

Jesus returned to heaven and pleads our name before His Father's throne, that one day we might join Him in Paradise.

It is with love that He abides with us still, and if we will but take His hand He will takes us unto himself when this earth we leave.

To be counted as one of His sheep is a gift of love that we all seek.

If we live but a day or a hundred years, we will never find a love greater than His.

When we close our eyes in death we will never have to fear, for the love of Jesus will see us through.

So while alive walk hand in hand with Jesus and proclaim His love to all that you meet.

Bless and keep His name always fresh in your heart and mind, and your heart will beat with love whenever His name is brought to mind.

Jesus Christ was, is, and always will be the one and only Son of God who came to earth to save a wretched soul such as me.

GLORY OF THE LORD

John 1:14
And the word became flesh and dwelt among us, and
we beheld His glory, the glory as of the only begotten
of the Father, full of grace and truth.

May my eyes see the glory of the Lord, my feet trod on
sacred ground.

May my eyes see the cross upon which my Lord died, may I
feel the anguish that my Lord bore for you and me.

He shed his blood so that it could cleanse us of our sins and set
us free.

A tainted heart cannot pass through the door of death and
enter heaven above.

A pure heart is surly a gift that we sinners do not deserve, but
due to Jesus' caring for you and me, He embellished us with his
love that day at Calvary.

Hold your head high and claim His victory before the day this
earth you leave.

Washed clean in the blood of the Lamb our souls will be when
we accept Jesus for who He claims to be.

Glory to God on high for accepting the sacrifice that Jesus
made on our behalf that day at Calvary.

For there is no other way for sinners such as you and me to
have a future where sin cannot abide.

Those streets of gold were paved for feet like yours and mine.

Jesus is that river of life that flows through the midst of heaven
and nourishes the soul.

In him and through Him is no darkness at all, just love for you
and me.

A love beyond our understanding, just waiting to be claimed by the repentant soul.

Praise God today, tomorrow, and always, for sending his Son, Jesus Christ, to die in our place on that cross at Calvary.

May the glory of the Lord shine roundabout and drive the temptations of sin away.

GOD LOVES US

John 15:12
This is my commandment, that you love one another as
I have loved you.

Follow almighty God, the one who created the mountains and the sea, He can lead us to a simpler life, one free from the burdens of today.

It matters not whether we like it or not, God is in complete control.

He knows our every thought and deed; He set us free to do as we please.

Some go astray and lose their way; others obey his every command and live His way.

To live by the open sea or on the open prairie is not as important as it is to live a life more pleasing to God.

Way too often we forget that God loves us and we do things that we would not do if we knew the consequences beforehand.

Our God is a loving God, and when we are through misbehaving, He welcomes us back with open arms.

When the end of life comes we are clothed in the webs that we have weaved, and upon these things we shall be judged by the God who created you and me.

We shall be judged by His standards, not ours. His rules of judging cannot be bent in any way.

Once we have confessed and repented of our sins before His throne we become to Him white as snow.

The restored soul praises God day and night and refresh themselves in His love.

God does love us and waits for us to see the error of our ways and return to Him with an open and contrite heart.

God's love will never fail, unlike man, God is perfect in every way and so is His love towards man.

Accept that love in your heart and your life will change and become more pleasing to God.

GOD'S GREAT LOVE

Deuteronomy 6:5
You shall love the Lord your God with all your heart,
with all your soul, and with all your strength.

May the Lord, Thy God, be with thee, may He uphold thee and strengthen thee.

In times of sickness, may He heal thee and give thee strength to endure the trials that face thee.

His grace abounds and can free thee from the sins that buffet thee.

Stand fast in His love and eternal life shall be thine.

Thou the dark shadows of death abound, fear not, for thy God will protect and comfort thee.

He will take thee unto His bosom and caress thee, and fill thine heart with joy.

Thy offspring shall prosper and bring glory to God's holy name.

You shall grow in the strength of the Lord day by day.

No harmful thing shall deter thee from seeking the Lord's face; neither shall you wander from his sheepfold.

Blessed be the name of the Lord, His love shall endureth forever.

As God put the stars in the heaven, so shall He endow man with the freedom of love.

Now and forevermore may God's love dwell in thine heart.

GOD'S HANDIWORK

Psalm 19:1
The heavens declare the glory of God, and the firmament shows His handiwork.

The planet upon which we live is but a speck of cosmic dust in a vast universe, it makes one complete revolution in twenty four hours and is hurtling through space at a speed of seventeen thousand five hundred miles per hour.

From the other side of the universe our planet is probably no larger than a period at the end of a sentence and yet as far as we know it is the only planet that is capable of supporting life.

Within this microcosm of dust, God has placed everything necessary to sustain life, from the fish of the sea to the trees and plants, an underground water supply and all else, that man will ever need.

Upon this planet, there are billions of people and wildlife traveling through space at an amazing rate of speed and yet everything stays in its given place.

Where is our planet headed? Has it changed its location in space since God put it in motion? How long will it sustain life?

Everything that God put on this planet was meant for the benefit of man, unfortunately in some cases man has depleted the natural resources that are at his disposal without regard for his fellowman.

Man has enslaved man as a natural resource and has taken advantage of his fellowman through exertion of power. Those responsible for the death of millions of people for monetary gain or political reasons will one day be held responsible and pay the price.

Little wonder the day will come when God will utterly destroy this our home in space because of the corruption that is steadily getting worse.

Those trying to promote God's kingdom here on earth are doing a great job, but this alone will not be enough to deter God's anger at the time of the end.

In the end times, this planet will be utterly destroyed and will no longer be a refuge in space for mankind.

God will have created a new planet where only the faithful followers of God and Jesus Christ will be allowed to live, all others will be cast into utter darkness, separated from God for all of eternity.

This new planet will be one where there will be no more sickness, disease, or death, even Satan will not be allowed to reside there and he will no longer have the power to tempt man to turn from God.

Man's new home will be far superior to what he now has and there will be no need of the sun or the moon to supply light, for God and Jesus shall be the light thereof and harmony will reign forevermore.

Are there other cosmic particles of dust out there like our planet or are we one of a kind? If so, do they support life as we know it? Are there other forms of life in God's creation? Some day we will know, but for now, we must accept God's creative powers as something that belongs to Him and Him alone.

No matter what, there is only one God, one savior (Jesus Christ), one Holy Ghost, and as each and everyone close their eyes in death, they will reopen them in a new world. One where all the secrets of God will be revealed and there will be no more questions.

GOD'S LOVE

John 14:14-15
If you ask anything in my name, I will do it. If you love
Me, keep My commandments.

We as humans think of love as affection one towards the other with intimate feelings involved.

We give gifts to try to influence or make a good impression on those to whom we give.

We expect something in return, whether it is loyalty or control over the one we shower with gifts.

God on the other hand gives to all without expecting anything in return; He gives because it is within His nature to give.

He gives us all varying gifts and they are the most precious gifts that we will ever receive.

Upon receiving gifts from God, we accept them as though we deserve them and jealously protect them from others.

When in fact we are not and never will be worthy enough to receive the gifts that God wants to bestow on us.

One of the greatest gifts is life itself, along with good health, our daily needs, and the ability of the body to heal itself.

God bestows upon us the gift of vision so that we can enjoy the beauty that surrounds us every day of our lives.

Hearing so that we may hear and heed His word when He speaks to us.

The sense of feeling, both physical and emotional, so that we can tell when our body needs attention and the ability to relate one to the other through our emotions.

All of our senses are a gift from God and serves to keep us in good standing with God and our neighbor.

God gives us the freedom of choice, freedom to choose how we will spend our days here on earth and a chance to serve Him.

The greatest gift of all we all too often take for granted and do not fully appreciate, God sent his Son, Jesus Christ, to be a sacrifice for the sins of the whole world, thus freeing us from the bondage of sin.

Without that sacrifice, we would not be able to approach the throne of God and seek his forgiveness for our trespasses against Him.

Through Jesus Christ, we are granted the gift of eternal life just by believing that Jesus is the Son of God and that only through Him can we obtain eternal life.

God showers his gifts upon the just and the unjust alike, it is we who either accept these gifts or reject them.

Even death of the flesh is a gift from God, for without death of the flesh we would not be able to achieve eternal life with God.

The more we live a Christ like life the more we become aware of the gifts that God showers upon us, we come to see beyond ourselves and put God first in our lives.

A negative life style keeps us from receiving what God wants for us, negativity blocks our insight into the things of the spirit, where receptivity opens us up to the gifts that God has for those who love Him.

God gave us all the same capabilities, but only a few get beyond self and self-interests to the point where they recognize and appreciate the gifts that God bestows upon them.

Self is one of our greatest obstacles to a better and more spiritual life; we have to prepare ourselves to receive before we can receive.

Self-discipline is one of our greatest achievements in life; it opens doors that ordinarily would stay closed.

All good gifts great or small come from God; wise is the man who uses his gifts for the good of his fellowman.

Take God's hand as He extends it in love, accept His gift of love as the most precious gift that you will ever receive and you will abide with Him throughout eternity.

GOD'S LOVE AND CARE

1 Peter 5:7
Cast all of your cares upon Him, for He cares for you.

A gentle rain awoke me last night as it pitter-pattered on the roof.

It watered the ground and washed the face of the flowers before forming rivulets and heading back to the sea.

Just as the rain watered God's creation, His love and care waters our soul and our bodies responds to its healing balm.

As the sun rose and warmed the earth, God's hand reached out and touched my heart and my life has never been the same.

Where I once chased the pot of gold at the end of the rainbow, I now seek God's love and care wherever it can be found.

He walks before me as I go through the trials of life and slowly I am becoming purified like fine gold.

He affords me shelter when Satan throws his fiery darts towards my heart and tries to entice me to fall apart.

No matter where I go, whether it is in the depths of the sea or the highest mountain, God prepares the way and I find rest in his loving arms.

Soaring high above the earth, I look down and see the grandeur of God's creation from sea to sea.

In the bowels of the earth I might find myself and yet I am not alone, for God is there keeping me from falling into the great abyss.

God lights my way and steadies my hand as age takes its toll, I find myself seeking His love and care before His throne.

The love and care of God is to my soul as the rain is to the face of the earth and no matter where I roam, God is there.

I cannot escape this earth and dwell in heaven until I accept God's Son as my Lord and Savior and allow him to bless my soul.

It was through God's love and care that I was born and it will be through God's love and care that I shall return unto Him when with this earth I am through.

GOD'S OMNIPENT HAND

Colossians 1:16
For by Him all things were created that are in heaven and that are on earth, visible and invisible, whether thrones or dominions or principalities or powers. All things were created through Him and for Him.

As I trod the earth day by day, I come to see God's omnipotent hand in everything that I see.

From the rising of the sun to the setting of the moon and the stars that fill the heaven above were put there by His mighty hand.

In the forest so green, the mountains so high, God's creation was meant to be enjoyed by man.

Even the grasses that feed the animals of the wild and the streams that quench their thirst was thought of first in God's infinite mind.

The paths that we trod were all laid out before the beginning of time.

The birds of the air that nest in the trees or on the ground are all part of God's plan.

Nothing was made in vain; everything has its place and purpose in the life of man.

Since the creation, man has wandered from land to land and traversed the heavens only to find that God is in everything that can be brought to mind.

God blessed us as He set us free to do whatever we please.

It is man who stumbles and falls, and refuses to obey God's commands and hides his face in shame.

Were man to follow God from birth to death he would be content to live a simple life and praise Him at every turn.

Sometime today or tomorrow, Jesus Christ shall return to claim His own.

When He comes all who wandered from the path He set will weep and gnash their teeth, for they will have no bright tomorrow's.

Left behind to face their tomorrows without hope and full of sorrows.

Those who lived by His word shall rise triumphantly and follow their creator as He leads them to the new world that lies beyond the mind of man.

There to live in peace and harmony, serving God with joy in all He commands.

GOD'S CALLING

Galatians 5:13
For you, brethren, have been called to liberty; only do not use liberty as an opportunity for the flesh, but through love serve one another.

For the past two years, we have had the privilege of having Grady Sowell, a called man of God for our pastor and friend.

Resisting the calling at first, but as time went on the calling got stronger and stronger until finally he answered the call to serve God.

He gave up a successful place in the construction field to answer his calling to serve God in whatever capacity He wanted.

We have come to love Rev. Grady Sowell and his wife Carolyn as a brother and sister in Christ, who were willing to give up whatever necessary to lead wherever God lead.

Even through tragedies in their own lives, they hung on to their faith and have overcome problems that few of us have had to face.

The life of a minister is not an easy life, with his devoted wife Carolyn by his side he has moved from place to place and has shared his vast knowledge about our Lord, Jesus Christ.

Jesus became the center of his life and has walked with him wherever he has served.

I am sure that he has had times when he has questioned the wisdom of his decision to give up a life of prosperity to serve God wherever God wanted him to go.

Such decisions are not easy to make, especially where there is a family involved, but we who are sitting on the outside think that he made the right decision.

We along with all of the other lives that he has touched in his ministry career are the beneficiaries of his vast knowledge and love for God and his family.

He has sown the seeds of faith wherever he has served and has had the privilege of seeing some of them sprout and grow into a loving relationship with God.

But, like all of us we sow the seeds and move on to new ground, not knowing how fruitful our efforts have been.

Rev. Grady has harvested crops planted by others and others will harvest crops planted by him, his wish is that it matters not who sows the seeds as long as God is the final recipient of his and others efforts.

It is with deep regret that we have to say good-by to Grady and Carolyn Sowell, we are the richer for what they have given to us.

Grady may think that he is going to go into permanent retirement, but we are sure that God has other plans for him; perhaps it is time for him to write about his experiences and his love for the Lord.

Once called it is a lifetime occupation, God will guide him and his wife Carolyn wherever they may go.

Thank you Brother Sowell for sharing your love for God with us. You will be sorely missed.

We the members of the Barton United Methodist Church wish you and Carolyn

God's speed and may you enjoy whatever the future holds for you both.

Note: Since this time both Brother Grady and Carolyn have gone on to be with Jesus. They will surely be missed by those whose lives they touched while in the ministry.

GOD'S THRONE

Hebrews 4:16
Let us therefore come boldly to the throne of grace,
that we may obtain mercy and find grace to help in
time of need.

Before the throne of God I prostate fall.

I bare my soul and ask forgiveness of my sins, one and all.

I heard someone knocking on my door; I opened it and found love and eternal life on the other side.

Whether I live many days or just a few, I will help my fellowman open that door too.

God has lead me by the hand and restored my soul so that I may spread His word while here on earth I remain.

He opened my eyes so that I might see His truths and help my fellowman.

It was while I was prostate before his throne that I come to know Him as my own.

It is with a humble heart and open mind that I seek the Lord's face and encourage my fellow sojourners to do the same.

Before the throne of God I prostate fall and give myself as an example to all.

GOD'S WAY

Jeremiah 31:33
But this is the covenant that I will make with the house
of Israel after those days, says the Lord; I will put My
law in their minds, and write it on their hearts; and I
will be their God, and they shall be My people.

If Christians around the world had their way, everyone would
come before the throne of God and receive forgiveness of their sins.

They would be raised above the temptations of Satan and
receive salvation which is a gift from God to man.

No one would lose their life through succumbing to the
pleasures of the flesh; God has prepared a way that all can be
washed white as snow.

God sent His Son, Jesus Christ, as a sacrifice for the sins of
man, and by accepting Jesus Christ as our Savior we too can be a
sheep of his pasture.

We can live through Jesus Christ, not of ourselves or what we
do or say, it is only through Jesus that we can receive the gift of
eternal life.

Christians must forgive all who have offended them and seek
forgiveness from those who they have offended.

Without forgiveness and forgiving, we are not fit to enter into
the kingdom of God.

Repentance covers our sins and never again will they be
brought against us, though they are as scarlet, they will become as
white as snow through the love of Jesus Christ.

If Christians had, their way sin would be a thing of the past
and never brought before man again.

Let God have His way in your life, come before Him and seek His face and assure your place in His kingdom, whether it be here on earth or in heaven above.

Through submission to God, the trials of this life will be made easier and our path will lead to eternal life with God.

God's way is the only way that anyone will ever be able to enter His kingdom and be spared from being thrown into the lake that burns with brimstone, along with all who reject Him.

GRACE AND LOVE

2 Corinthians 12:9
And he said to me, "My grace is sufficient for you, for My strength is made perfect in weakness." Therefore most gladly I will rather boast in my infirmities, that the power of Christ may rest upon me.

My sins brought me to the foot of the cross where I accepted the redemptive work of Jesus Christ.

As Jesus hung on that cross at Calvary, He suffered beyond human endurance so that you and I might be freed from the bondage of sin.

Jesus was a sacrifice for the sins of the world, no other would do, He was the only one strong enough to endure.

As His life slipped away, the veil in the temple tore in two, from the ceiling to the floor it tore.

This opened the Holy of Holies to the common man and gave him access to God.

Jesus is calling for all to gather around the cross and bare witness that He still has grace and love for all who believe.

Like the great shepherd that He is He will lead his flock to green pastures and wipe their tears away.

He will protect them from the ravaging wolves that line their way from birth to the separation of the body from the soul.

While they live here on earth, He will supply all of their needs, from the clothes on their backs to the food that they eat and the roof that protects them from the heat and the cold.

Our Lord stands on the highest hill for all of the world to see, He hides not His grace and love from any man.

He writes their sins in the book of life towards the great day of judgment, but if they repent of their sins He throws it all away.

His love and grace will endure forever, through sunshine and rain, and is sufficient for everyone today if unto Him they pray.

GROWTH IN THEE

Revelation 3:20
Behold, I stand at the door and knock. If anyone hears
my voice and opens the door, I will come into him and
dine with him, and he with Me.

Almighty God, creator of the universe and all things
therein.

Grant us freedom from Satan and free us from our evil
thoughts and deeds, direct our lives to the benefit of our
fellowman.

Grant that we will hold Thee in the highest esteem, and follow
that still small voice within.

The voice that tells us right from wrong, the voice of the Holy
Spirit that dwells within us all.

Father, You allow evil to exist only to show that through
adversity we can grow strong when we resist the temptations that
befall us.

When we turn to our Lord, Jesus Christ, and accept Him as
the Son of God, then do we feel the strength within us to resist evil
and triumph over evil.

Peace shall prevail where the love of God has entered the life of
those who believe.

Father, we humble ourselves before Thy throne and seek
forgiveness of our sins and ask that You be with us in all that we do
and say.

Heavenly Father, keep us from stumbling as we live our lives in
service to You and Your kingdom here on earth.

We thank Thee that we can come to You in our times of need
and find comfort and peace for our troubled souls.

As we grow in age, may we also grow in the knowledge of Thee, and be prepared to join Thee when this life we leave.

Grant us our petitions O Lord; grant us the power to resist the evil one as he tries to ensnare us in the temptations of the flesh.

These things we pray in the name of Thy Son, Jesus Christ, A-men.

GUIDE AND DIRECT

2 Corinthians 5&
For we walk by faith, not by sight.

Be with us Lord God as we walk this pathway of life.

Keep us from stumbling over the rocks of sin that are on this pathway.

Walk close O Lord, so that we might touch the hem of Your garment when sickness and disease overtakes us.

Through the dark of night may Your guiding "Light" illuminate our way as we wander through the wilderness and arid areas of life.

Touch the heart of the unrepentant so that they might see the error of their ways and turn to Thee.

To those who are deaf, unlock their ears so that they might hear Thy words and come before Thy throne in humbleness of heart.

As Thy secrets are unlocked through understanding, grant us the courage and desire to bring Your message of salvation to the lost.

For once, we were the lost and brothers in Christ brought us the message of salvation.

We give Thee thanks O Lord for Your creation and for the day that we will be free from the tethers of this life and abide with Thee for eternity.

This is the fervent prayer of all who accept Jesus Christ as Thy one and only Son.

THOSE WHO REACH OUT TO OTHERS

Romans 8:27
Now He who searches the hearts knows what the mind of the spirit is, because He makes intercession for the saints according to the will of God.

Heavenly Father we who are about to enter into a new venture turn to Thee and ask for Your guidance.

We ask that You guide and keep us as we reach out to those who need a helping hand.

May we always keep You foremost in our thoughts and deeds.

Let us not forget that it was us who at one time needed Your help to overcome our hardships.

May we express compassion where compassion is needed and not condemn our fellowman for his shortcomings.

If there be any doubt or dishonesty in this undertaking, let it surface now and be corrected before it becomes a stumbling block.

We ask that You provide us with the knowledge and wisdom to guide this organization in its efforts to provide for the ones who will be seeking our help.

Give us the wisdom to choose our fellow workers wisely, so that they too might reflect Your love and compassion towards the less fortunate.

When difficulties do arise, may we be wise in the decisions that we will be called upon to make.

Bless all who will come together to do Your will in providing services towards the advancement of Your kingdom here on earth.

It is a great undertaking and can only be successful if You are the center of our endeavors.

Though there will be many obstacles to be overcome, we will fear not as long as You keep Your hand on our lives.

Though we will benefit greatly ourselves, may Your guiding hand always be upon us and keep our benefits from becoming the reason for why we are doing our jobs.

To serve You, Almighty God, is the reason that we are willing to face the criticism and challenges that we will face from the secular world.

Guide us as we endeavor to handle some of the wealth of this world to the benefit of our fellowman.

Bless those who have contributed a portion of their wealth so that others might live a more enterprising life and contribute to Your kingdom here on earth.

Bless and protect all who step forth in faith to commit their lives so that others might benefit from their endeavors.

We ask You once again to prepare the way so that we might reach out in a loving way and that we might have compassion towards our fellowman.

With Your help and only through Your help can such an endeavor be successful, to this end we commit our time and lives.

We humbly come before Thy throne and commit our lives to Thy service, now and forevermore.

HAVE YOU TALKED
WITH GOD TODAY

Luke 18:1
Then He spoke a parable to them, that men always
ought to pray and not lose heart.

As I walked the shore, I came across a conch shell rolling in
the waves as they broke upon the shore.

Wading out in the breaking surf, I bent over and cradled it in
my hands.

Holding it to my ear, this is what I heard, "Have you talked
with God today? I have."

Not quite believing what I heard, I shook my head and smiled
inside.

Again, I put the conch shell to my ear, this time I heard the
surf breaking upon the shore.

It reminded me of days of old when I was young and frolicked
in the surf, playing tag with each receding sea.

I recalled the sails of old as they silently glided by, heading to
foreign lands, far beyond where the sea met the sky.

Days of fog too thick to see the breaking surf, but hear it, I
could in the conch shell as I held it to my ear.

Coming back to where I now stood, I again held the conch
shell to my ear and this is what I heard, "Have you talked with God
today? I have."

A way of God to remind me that every day I should bow my
head and pray.

"Yes, I have talked with God today. Have You?"

HE DIED FOR YOU AND ME

Romans 5:8
But God demonstrates His own love towards us, in that
while we were still sinners, Christ died for us.

My most fervent prayer is that you have had or will have a
personal relationship with Jesus Christ, for only through Jesus can
we be saved.

It is only through Jesus Christ that we will be able to enjoy one
another in heaven above.

Jesus paid our debt for sin when he died upon the cross at
Calvary.

While on the cross, Jesus finished the work that He came to
earth to do and when He did this great service for mankind He had
you and me in mind.

Jesus never ran from His responsibilities and neither should we.

All He asks us to do is to tell all we meet what He has done for
you and me.

He is a great one to know, He has a gift for all who choose to
bend their knees before His throne and accept Him as their Lord
and King. For the Son of God is He.

Even Jesus' enemies knew that He was the Son of God, but
they refused to accept Him for who he claimed to be, because
they feared that they would lose the power and authority that they
claimed to have.

Though Jesus had the power to create and destroy He never
used it while here on earth, for His purpose of coming was to open
the door to heaven for all who would and will believe.

When Jesus returns to earth, He will claim his own and trod
on those who refuse to call Him their own.

With his mighty hand, He will bind Satan and all others who stubbornly refuse to bend their knees before His throne.

With tears in His eyes He will condemn the wicked to the Lake of Fire, where the worm never dies.

It is here and now that man can avoid the condemnation and live a life pleasing to God and man.

HE GUIDES ME

2 Corinthians 12:9
And He said to me, "My grace is sufficient for you, for My strength is made perfect in weakness." Therefore most gladly I will rather boast in my infirmities, that the power of Christ may rest upon me.

I can go forward when I am steeped in His doctrine and wrapped in His love.

He will guide me as I travel from place to place, spreading His word as I go.

From the highest mountain to the depths of the sea, He sends me, guided from above.

Love and peace is my message, eternal life is my reward.

Where once I was a sinner, now I am a saint, guided and blessed by God every step of the way.

Once not knowing from whence I came, now I know the whole story, as told in the pages of His written word.

God has granted me grace as through the trials of this life I have trod, even as weary as sometimes I am.

His love has sustained me; His light has saved me from the sins that had bound me.

Where once I was lost, now I rest in His arms of love, waiting for Him to part the waters so that I might pass through.

All of the sins that try to engulf me are swept away by His cleansing waters, when on the shore of life I stand.

From the rising of the sun to the setting of the moon, I fear no evil, for God is guiding me and protecting me from the snares of the fouler (Satan).

His love is like the rising of the sun, it is always there to warm my soul and let me know that He loves me all the day through.

With you, I share what God has blessed me with, a guiding hand, an encouraging word, and a love that understands.

Blessed is the one who seeks God, for the day will come when they will need a guiding hand, seek Him and live forever in His loving arms.

HE IS CALLING

Isaiah 55:6
Seek the Lord while He may be found, call upon Him
while He is near.

I hear the voice of God calling me home and I cannot resist the voice of the one who created me.

He has seen me through the trials of this life that I had to endure; He never left me on my own.

He comforted me when all seemed to be lost, through His love and care I survived.

Though I fell short of what God intended for me to be, He still loved and cared for me.

This life is a journey that God laid out for me and He gave me a choice to follow him or turn the other way.

When I disobeyed, He allowed me to live life my way until I saw the error of my ways.

Then He held his arms wide and I ran to the comfort of His side.

God is calling and I must obey, for He knows what is best for me.

In the distance, I can see the "Light" that drives all sin away and in that "Light" is where I want to be.

CHOSEN

1 Peter 5:6
Therefore humble yourself under the mighty hand of
God, that He may exalt you in due time.

In the books of the Bible, I have found words of love and
wisdom.

There are words to guide the wayward and bring peace to a
wretched soul.

It is as though they were written yesterday, some two thousand
years or more ago.

No matter when they were written they were all inspired by the
same Master of our soul.

He reached down with His mighty hand and guided the pen of
many a man since time began.

It makes one humble and proud inside to know that God chose
them to tell the story of His love for man.

The one who writes for money shall his pockets fill, but the one
who writes for God will be doing "His will".

We as writers will never know where our words will go, but we
pray that one day they will comfort the heart of a sinner and heal
their soul.

It is to God that the glory shall go, for without Him this pen
would be silent and still.

He guides the pen every time it is in the hand of a writer who
wants to spread the words of comfort.

Glory is to God for raising writers who submit to their calling
and ask not for gold or silver, just the chance to pen a few words
that can comfort a troubled soul.

The words penned for the flesh will soon pass away, but the words penned through the guidance of God shall endure for all time.

Thank you God for including my name on the list of writers that you have chosen for such an honorable task.

HE TOUCHED ME

John 8:36
Therefore if the Son make you free, you shall be free
indeed.

Since Jesus touched me, I am not the man I used to be.

He touched me with his hand and set me free from the sins
that blinded me.

What a joy it is to be free to help my fellowman to see that the
way to eternal life is through the man who set me free.

As long as I live, I will always be grateful to God for sending
His Son, Jesus Christ, to open my eyes so that I could see.

From the time that I was young, Jesus has had His hand on me.

From the cradle to the grave, He has and will look after me.

It seems like only yesterday that Jesus healed me as He did his
followers many long years ago.

Jesus still reaches across space and time and sets us free, oh
what a friend He has been to me.

Jesus has filled my life with the things that last for eternity.

I no longer have a list of wants, He has replaced my wants with
His love and that is what life is all about to me.

Freedom comes to all who seek His will and obey His
commands; He supplies our every need.

Yes, since Jesus touched me I am not the man I used to be.

I go about with a smile on my face, extending a helping hand
to those I meet, what a difference Jesus has made in me.

Joy, joy is all I see since Jesus touched me; the sins of the old
man no longer interest me. Like a child, I listen and obey what
Jesus has to say.

Merrill Phillips

I may stumble, but never again will I go astray, for Jesus' love sustains me and guides me along the way.

From your healing "Light" to the forgiveness of my sins I thank you Lord Jesus for everything you have done for a sinner like me.

HEAL US WE PRAY

Matthew 10:8
Heal the sick, cleanse the lepers, raises the dead, cast
out demons. Freely you have received, freely give.

Holy Father, creator of us all, hear our petitions as we bring
the names of the sick and ill before Thy throne.

Touch each and everyone so that they might feel Thy love and
healing hand in their times of need.

Those who lie in hospitals with an uncertain future, give them
hope through Thy Son, Jesus Christ.

He lit the "Light" of freedom within our hearts and stands at
the door knocking.

To whoever will open that door and let Him in will receive
blessings beyond their expectations.

Heavenly Father you supply our needs even before we know
what they are.

It is with an open mind and heart that we come before You and
offer ourselves to Thy service.

Enable us O Lord to go forth and proclaim Thy love and
healing power to all that we meet.

Grant us the strength and courage to carry out Thy will in our
lives and be Your ambassadors to all we meet.

Touch our lives in ways that we will know without a doubt that
it was You who prompted us to speak the truth in Thy name.

Through Thy loving touching hand, we will and can be healed
of all of our infirmities, great and small.

We come to Thee in the name of Thy Son, Jesus Christ. A-men

HELP US

Psalm 46:1
God is our refuge and strength. A very present help in trouble.

Oh heavenly Father, God above, help us to become more like You.

Help us to know that no matter the circumstances we can come to You through prayer and find comfort.

Quiet our fears as we go through life day by day, may we grow closer to You as we seek to do Thy will.

May our walk on the straight and narrow way be fruitful throughout our days.

Oh, Lord may we submit to Thy will and find comfort as we spread your word.

Like the patriarchs of old who shouldered their cross and followed You, may we of today take up our cross and do the same.

Open our eyes and fill our hearts with thoughts of You so that we might pass on to others Your words that ring so true.

Bless and keep us O Lord we pray, keep us from going astray and losing sight of You.

When we draw our last breath here on earth, may we awaken in Thy presence and begin life anew with Thee.

HELPING HAND

Lamentations 3:26
It is good that one should hope and wait quietly for the
salvation of the Lord.

Through the power of Jesus Christ, we can go forth into this
hurting world and express His love through ourselves.

No matter where we might travel, there is an opportunity to
express heavenly love.

Just showing courtesy by holding a door for someone or
wishing them a nice day we express love for our fellowman.

It takes only a moment to make someone's life a little more
bearable, it may even change their whole outlook on life and its
problems.

It is a wise man who errs on the side of love rather than
expressing a negative attitude.

How many times have you seen someone put somebody down,
rather than building them up with a complement?

All too often, we act in a negative way when it would have been
just as easy to express love.

Negative thinking can build to the point of carrying out an act
of violence.

To set an example for others to follow is what is asked of all
who believe, deeds without faith or to impress others is folly.

Test all doctrine against scripture before blindly indulging in a
doctrine that could lead you astray.

Live your life so as others can see Jesus in what you say and do.

Do not speak out of the side of your mouth, for whatever you
say or do you will be held accountable on the Day of Judgment.

In helping others you help yourself to grow in your ability to express God's love.

A helping hand will be as welcomed as a gentle spring rain, as the rain supplies the flower of the field with nourishment, so can a helping hand help revive a saddened heart.

HIS CLEANSING "LIGHT"

Psalm 27:1
The lord is my light and my salvation; whom shall I
fear? The Lord is the strength of my life; of whom shall
I be afraid?

The Lord is my light and my salvation; whom shall I fear?

How sweet it is to depend upon the truths that God has revealed to me.

When in times of trouble I can call upon them to see me through.

The day before I believed I was lost in sin and could not see.

The light of God that removes the darkness of sin shined upon me.

No shadow did it cast where sin could hide, the light of God had come to set me free.

How sweet it was the first day that I believed, I felt God's love enter my heart and drive the temptations of sin away.

Though I still remember the sins I indulged in, they no longer keep me from my Savior's side.

Where my feet once trod the pathway to hell, they now follow the pathway to heaven where Jesus abides.

With my hand in His I will never again fall prey to sin, nor be enticed to turn my back on the one who created me.

God's love is the only thing that we need to set us free.

HIS GREAT CREATION

Colossians 1:16
For by Him all things were created that are in heaven and that are on earth, visible and invisible, whether thrones or dominions or principalities or powers. All things were created through Him and for Him.

Wow, what a place God created when He made the earth, a place for His children to live and play.

He filled it full of treasures for those who have a curious mind and a desire to explore.

For those who seek peace and quiet God created high mountains and secret places where few travel.

He created arid places where only the hearty dwell.

God created the mighty oceans and filled them with an abundant supply of sea creatures to satisfy the appetite of man.

The forests of the world are of his handiwork too, from the stately cedars of Lebanon to the mighty redwoods, and in these forests He placed a great variety of wild beasts, all for the pleasure of man.

Great swamps and jungles that are scattered hither and yon all hold treasures for those who are hearty enough to enter therein.

The spectacular views from the tops of the highest mountains to the depths of the deepest seas holds man in awe of God's creative hand.

In the heavens above God placed the stars and the planets that greet us when the sun goes down and darkness prevails.

Man is not content to just roam the world at hand; he must explore the heavens above to seek out the mysteries of God's creative hand.

When the sun rises, above the eastern horizon, it awakens millions of sleeping souls and they go about like little children racing to and fro.

Mighty rivers rush towards the sea and yet the seas are never full, nor do the rivers run dry.

Everything that man uses or sees was created by God's mighty hand, His love for man is boundless and so should our love for God be.

God asks no questions, nor does He hold anything back, it is God's world and yet He gave it all to man.

Learn to love and respect this world that God created and when hard times come it will take care of you and provide all that is needed to see you through.

HIS HAND WILL GUIDE US

Psalm 31:14-16
But as for me, I trust in You, O Lord; I say, "You are my God." My times are in Your hand; deliver me from the hand of my enemies, and from those who persecute me. Make Your face shine upon Your servant; save me for your mercies sake.

Heavenly Father with Your guiding hand we can survive all circumstances, whether it be disease unto death or healing unto life.

You are with us no matter where the road of life leads us.

If we obey Thy signs along the way, we can live a less sinful life, enabling us to spread Your word wherever we may roam.

From the rising of the sun to the setting of the moon You are ever present and ready to intervene in our lives if we so ask.

Your love encompasses all people, regardless of their color or creed.

At a moment's notice You will inject Your healing love in our lives if our hearts are in a receptive mode.

From the cradle to the grave, You are ready, willing, and able to help us overcome any and all adversity that might stand between us.

We thank You O Lord God for providing us a way to overcome sin (no matter what it might be) through Thy Son, Jesus Christ.

Through his name, we petition Thee O God that Thy will may be done in our lives.

In the name of the Father, Son, and Holy Ghost, A-men.

HIS MIGHTY HAND

Ephesians 2:10
For we are his workmanship, created in Christ Jesus for good works, which God prepared beforehand that we should walk in them.

I live within the realm of God in safety; He protects me from the fiery darts of Satan.

Without Him I can do nothing, feel nothing, and shall surly be cast into everlasting hell.

Though the jaws of death threaten me, I tremble not, for God holds my hand.

With each sunrise comes a new day, granted by God, and with it life is renewed.

With the rising of the moon the wonders of heaven are displayed, God's mighty creative power is revealed in all its splendor.

Just as the stars reveal God's creative hand, so is His love revealed to me.

Peace is to those who obey His commandments and looks upon his neighbor as a child of God.

From the fruit of the trees to the rolling seas, God reveals Himself to all who believe.

God's warehouses are full to overflowing, just waiting for us to claim our inheritance.

The floodgates of hell shall not prevail against the awesome power of our Creator, God.

God tolerates Satan because he was created by God, though he will be cast into the lake of fire he is still loved by his Creator, God.

And the same applies to many of us, God loves us and yet those who rebel against God shall join Satan in his eternal torment.

From all corners of the globe, evil shall rise against God and threaten eternal peace and love, but in the twinkling of an eye, fire shall come down from heaven and destroy the last bastions of evil and peace shall reign forever and ever.

Under the mighty hand of God, all of these things shall come to pass, and the faithful shall fear not, for God has prepared a place in paradise for all who stand fast and fail not in the sight of God.

HIS SHELTERING WINGS

Psalm 36:7
How precious is your loving kindness, O God!
Therefore the children of men put their trust under the
shadow of Your wings.

Dear Lord I am here to ask that Thy will be done here on
earth.

May your grace abound and Your light shine upon our pathway
of life today and forever.

We praise Thee and seek Thy sheltering wings when the storms
of life buffet us and sin tries to lead us astray.

O Lord that You will walk before us night and day with Thy
loving arms around us we pray.

As we travel from the mountains to the sea go before us O
Lord, for without You surly we will go astray.

In the dark of night when all seems lost, may Thy light shine
upon our path and light the way.

Take the fear of death away as leave this life and begin life
anew with Thee one day.

HISTORY REPEATS ITSELF

Mark 15:12-13
Pilate answered and said to them again, "What then do
you want me to do with Him whom you call the King
of the Jews?" So they cried again, "Crucify Him!"

God, being the loving God that He is allows us to have
our own way, for He gave us the freedom of choice and will never
interfere in our decisions in life unless we ask Him to.

But what is forgotten by rebellious children is the fact that
there are consequences for rebellious decisions.

As there were consequences for crucifying Jesus in Biblical
times so are there consequences today for rejecting Jesus.

The voices of rebellious people are the same now as they
were then.

Oh how sad God must be about those who reject Jesus today as
they did in ancient times.

One day God will show His disapproval by ending life here on
earth as we know it today.

Then it will be too late to turn the pages of time backwards and
try to change ones ways and actions.

Disobedient children never seem to change until some tragic
event happens in their lives and they have no other place to turn for
comfort except God.

History does repeat itself, but that doesn't mean that we cannot
learn from our past mistakes and make adjustments in our lives so
that we will be able to receive the love that God has to offer.

HOLY GUIDANCE

Acts 2:4
And they were all filled with the Holy Spirit and began to speak with other tongues, as the Spirit gave them utterance.

Thank you Lord Jesus for giving us the Holy Spirit to be our comforter before You ascended into heaven after Your resurrection.

From the prophets of old to the Holy Spirit we of this world have had someone to guide us, as generation after generation has inhabited this earth.

God in His infinite wisdom has always had His hand on the pulse of mankind.

No matter in which generation any of us has lived we have always had a spiritual representative in whom we could call upon when in need.

As you O God intended for man to live forever, and so shall it be, You have made our existence easier by providing spiritual guidance.

It is only fitting that we of this generation pay homage for Your generosity of supplying us with the love and guidance of the Holy Spirit.

From Adam to the last person to live on planet earth has been under the guidance of a spiritual counterpart.

Your Son, Jesus Christ, was and is our atoning sacrifice for our sins, and balm to heal all stripes, and we who follow You are very grateful.

"Thanks" is so little to say for having been given so much, as a follower I too humble myself before Thy throne and swear allegiance to Your doctrines and will endeavor to spread Your word as the opportunity arises.

In order for Your love to be effective in this world it must be passed from one generation to the next through word and example.

This is mostly done by those who You select from one generation to the next to spread Your word so that no one will have an excuse for not coming to know You.

We who believe in Your doctrine look forward to the day when Your Son, Jesus Christ, returns and claims His own and abides with us in the new world of Your making.

Through Your Holy guidance O God, we of this generation will do our best to see to it that Your word and doctrine will survive the onslaught of Satan and remain a loving influence on those who will come after us, to this end we pledge our lives.

HOPE

Romans 5:3-5
And not only that, but we also glory in tribulations, knowing that tribulation produces perseverance; and perseverance, character; and character, hope. Now hope does not disappoint, because the love of God has been poured out in our hearts by the Holy Spirit who was given to us.

Father God, thou knoweth our days on earth, may we fulfill them pleasing to You.

You have showered us with all that we need, our cup over followeth.

Yet we find it hard to give up our loved ones, even though we know they now reside with Thee.

Precious are their memories and the times that we spent together, but now they have gone on to their greater rewards.

Rewards given of you, Almighty God, given for the services that they rendered unto You while here on earth.

We cherished the encouragement that they showed towards us while we were growing to maturity.

Now it is we who are of the older generation, may we encourage our offspring as we were encouraged by those who have gone on before us.

Years are like fleeting shadows, they pass all too quickly, it was just yesterday that we were young, and now it is near time for us to lay our heads down in death and return to You.

The time to secure our future with Thee is now, for once we close our eyes in death we shall stand before Thee and be assigned our destination according as to how we lived our lives here on earth.

Life and death is in the hands of our Almighty God, He chooses our number of days and assigns us the way that we should live.

He leaves to us the choice as to how we live our lives, and in the same context He rewards us accordingly.

Father, as we began life as innocent lambs of Thy flock, so may we end our days in peace and in the knowledge that we have lived according to Thy ways, and if it be Thy will, may we spend eternity with Thee.

HOW TO LIVE

Philippians 2:21
For to me, to live is Christ, and to die is gain.

Whether I live or die is not as important as to how I live my life.

A life apart from God is an idle life without hope.

Following God and seeking His will can produce success beyond belief.

To be puffed up with self-achievement can destroy what one starts out in life to accomplish.

Humbling one's self before the throne of God in meekness and adoration buries self, thus allowing the attributes of God to shine through.

To second guess God, is folly and results in an un-fulfilling life.

As the seeds of self-accomplishment surface deny them lest you overshadow your calling and end up empty.

Glorify God and put Him first in all that you do and you will prosper.

Work not for God and desire self-achievement, for it is detrimental to your spiritual growth.

It would be better to live a life of poverty and have a close relationship with God than to have the riches of this world that can replace God in your life.

Peace comes to those who give up self and seek God's will in their lives.

Though God wants us to have the best things in life, He sometimes holds them from us because He knows that we will let them get in the way of our relationship with Him.

God knows us better than we know ourselves, He knows that we are weak and easily lead astray.

This life is full of temptations, many of which can be detrimental to our final destination of spending eternity with God.

This life can be very productive to the advancement of God's kingdom here on earth if we are willing to give up self and follow what God wants for our lives.

God will bring His children together to be members of His Church and for the advancement of His will and when we leave this life, we will take our place in heaven that He has kept for us from the beginning of time.

A life of doing God's will or a life of disobedience is everyone's choice and there are rewards for both.

To follow God assures us of our heavenly home, to choose to be disobedience will lead us to spending eternity in hell.

HUMBLE EXPECTATIONS

1Peter 5:6
Therefore humble yourselves under the mighty hand of God, that he may exalt you in due time.

We as poets and writers for God pray to almighty God for guidance when our pens we take in hand.

We offer to God our writings as a tribute for the love that He bestows upon us as we follow His guiding hand.

We wait patiently for Him to stir our souls and bring to mind what He wants us to say.

As it has been said, "The world is not big enough to hold all that could be written about God and His love for man".

It takes a devoted soul to do the will of God without the expectation of monetary reward.

It is sufficient reward to spread His word and love to all who are willing to listen and encourage us to keep writing.

To plant the seeds of salvation in the hearts of the lost, for we too were at one time lost until God touched our lives and called us to serve.

We writers of the word write out of a labor of love and put God first in our lives, we are willing to sacrifice and live a quiet life to show our appreciation for what He has done for us.

We plow the ground and plant the seed so that others might water the word and even others reap the rewards, just as long as God is glorified in all that we do.

It is better to serve the Lord in love and lay up treasures in heaven than it is to deny His calling and face an uncertain future.

If you have a poet or writer among you who is doing the will of God, support him or her in whatever way you are lead.

I BELIEVE

Hebrews 11:6
But without faith it is impossible to please Him, for he who comes to God must believe that He is, and that He is a rewarder of those who diligently seek Him.

I believe in a triune God, God the father, God the Son, and God the Holy Spirit (or Holy Ghost).

God has set forth certain laws and instruction for us to live by and it is up to each individual to either accept or reject these laws and instruction.

By rejecting these laws and instructions does not make anyone any less of a child of God.

What does happen if one rejects these laws and instructions is that they live outside of the protection of God and face damnation when this life they leave.

As much as God loves us, He will respect and abide by our decision to either live a life according to His laws or the temptations of Satan.

Satan is the prince of this world and possesses the power of temptation and will do all that he can to get us to succumb to his temptations.

As persuasive, as Satan's temptations may be we (you and I) have the protection of Jesus Christ to help us deny the temptations of Satan.

One must remember that Jesus is supreme in this world and has power way beyond the abilities of Satan and will help us deny Satan if we ask Him to.

By succumbing to the temptations of Satan, we separate ourselves from the protection that Jesus offers and thus we fall prey to Satan's wishes.

But at any time in our lives we can overcome Satan's temptations by seeking Jesus Christ and asking Him to come into our lives and be our Lord and Master.

Through the study of the scriptures of the Bible and an open mind and heart, we can build a shield of truth that we can use whenever we are tempted by Satan.

It is we ourselves who determines whether we will obey the temptations of Satan or follow the ways of Jesus Christ; this is a freedom that God has granted us.

Only God is supreme and has the power to create or destroy, Satan can only tempt, he is like a roaring lion without any teeth.

Satan's temptations may seem to have power and authority, but they can be overcome through the truths that Jesus Christ has provided us.

Even in a lifetime we cannot fully understand the ways of God, it is incumbent upon us to accept the truths of God by faith and a personal relationship with His Son, Jesus Christ.

Jesus will reveal these truths a little at a time, as we are capable of understanding them and implementing them in our lives.

To be granted too much understanding all at once would certainly overwhelm us, like babies, we receive the milk of God a little at a time until we become capable of understanding the deep things of God.

By this method, we grow slowly and form a solid foundation upon which to build our lives of servitude to God.

As we grow and serve, we gain wisdom and thus we are capable of reaching out to our fellowman and help him in his efforts to understand and live by the truths of God.

Through growth, we gain a greater insight into the spiritual realm of life and come to realize that this life is a constant struggle between good and evil and how much we need the guidance of a triune God, God the Father, God the Son, and God the Holy Ghost.

NEED YOU JESUS

Matthew 6:8
Therefore do not be like them. For your Father knows
the things you have need of before you ask him.

Lord Jesus I beseech You through the Holy Ghost to quiet my fears and grant me peace.

When things go wrong I know that You walk beside me and when the storms of life rage You are near to my troubled soul.

In the dark of night when I cannot sleep, comfort me as I try to turn my problems over to You.

We come short of praising You when thing go wrong and our lives are full of woe.

I remember times when You have kept me from harm and I never recognized Your presence until later on.

My greatest desire is to do your will O Lord, but many times earthly things come between You and me, and for a while I lose my thoughts of You.

Guide me in the right direction, O Lord, open the doors that I might see the path that You have laid before me.

It isn't easy to keep going as I am, but with Your guiding hand I can and will follow You till You take me home.

The day fast approaches when I will not be able to continue as I am today, but when that day arrives, I pray that You will take my hand and lead the way.

With Your guidance may the words that You have given me to say be found in print to help others even more than I do today.

Guide me O Lord, guide me in the direction that You want me to go, and I will follow.

TEARS OF LOVE

John 7:38
He who believes in Me, as the Scripture has said, out of
his heart will flow rivers of living waters.

Did you ever think of rain as being God's tears over the disobedience of man or the wind that drives the rain as the breath of God?

God waters the face of the earth and his breath dries our tears.

It is God and God alone who can heal the ills of man.

With his mighty hand, God created the universe and all that is therein, without Him nothing was made.

A lifetime here on earth is not time enough to learn all that there is to learn about God, so from generation to generation we pass on to others what we have learned.

In hopes that the next generation will take up where we left off and advance their knowledge of God to the benefit of all.

Perhaps this is a reason why so much time has passed from Adam and Eve to the present time and the end of the age.

God in His mysterious ways controls all that goes on and allows things to happen that we think are contrary to His ways and yet in the long run they glorify Him.

As the tears of God's love flow let us come before Him and become an instrument by which His love is spread from generation to generation.

When the rain wets your face, remember that it is God's way of reminding you that He loves you and wants to wash all of your sins away.

THANKS

Romans 12:16
Be of the same mind towards one another. Do not
set your mind on high things, but associate with the
humble. Do not be wise in your own opinion.

Thanks is a word too often forgotten, whether it be in our
daily lives or in our prayers to God.

When being corrected for our wrongs, a simple thanks can heal
many a harm.

Thanks shows our humbleness when against us things go
wrong.

Thanks can put us back in tune with God when on bended
knee we pray.

Thanks will never do any harm; it is a bridge to changing an
enemy into a friend.

Thanks can open the heart to healing when in sin we lie.

Thanks can stop a disagreement if verbally we express our
thanks to our marriage partner when in matters we disagree.

Thanks is one of those words that can restrain us when in
thought we want to wish someone harm.

T—Think of God before you express yourself.

H—Have a nice day.

A—Ask God for forgiveness of your sins.

N—Never retire for the night with anger in your heart.

K—Know that you are a child of God and live accordingly.

S—Save time each day for prayer.

THE LOWLY

Matthew 10: 24
A disciple is not above his teacher, nor a servant above
is master.

Throughout time God has used some of the most unlikely people to carry out His will here on earth, He chooses those who society considers as outcasts so far as standards of man are concerned.

Moses was a keeper of herds and well into old age and yet God called upon him to lead His people out of the land of Egypt.

Though Moses made all kinds of excuses as to why he was not the right one to carry out what God wanted him to do, God persisted and gave Moses the ability to carry out his calling.

Noah was also a man of older age and yet he was called upon to build the ark so as to preserve a remnant of man and animals that God inhabited the earth with.

God then proceeded to destroy everything and everybody on the face of the earth because of the corruption of mankind.

David was the youngest of many brothers and yet God called upon him to become one of the greatest kings of all times.

Though he strayed and became involved in deception and murder God still used him in His establishing the line from which our Lord and Savior, Jesus Christ, would emerge from.

The prophets of old were men who were not of the ruling class of people, they were lowly people who had a great love for God and were willing to be used by Him.

The Shepherds were considered to be the outcasts of society and God told them the great news that the Savior of the world had been born before anyone else knew about the birth of Jesus Christ.

When Jesus began His ministry, He chose fishermen, tax collectors, and most unlikely people to become His disciples, Jesus even selected the one who would betray Him as one of His disciples.

Paul was called upon to spread the gospel of Jesus Christ and before that he was one of the greatest persecutors of the followers of Jesus that there was at that time.

And so it has gone throughout the history of mankind, God calls those who are the most unlikely to promote His kingdom here on earth.

The educated and ones in power are too involved in their lifestyle to give up everything and follow a life of servitude to God.

Perhaps it is because the lowly people that God uses have nothing to lose and all to gain and are willing to follow Jesus because their minds are not closed to new ideas and ways of improving themselves.

It does take an open mind and an open heart to accept Jesus Christ and all that He stands for to model one's life after Him in order to be of service to Him.

Once in service to Jesus Christ comes great rewards, such as, peace, love for ones fellowman, forgiveness of offenses against us, compassion, self-discipline, and many other attributes of God.

There are many today who God has called upon to serve Him, many accept their calling and live lowly lives of servitude and are among those who throughout the centuries have been willing to serve God without thought of gain for themselves.

Why God chooses those whom He chooses to serve Him is known only to Him, He prepares them and supplies them with all that they need to carry out their calling.

Whether ancient times or modern times God uses the lowly to bring the good news of Salvation to the four corners of the earth and reserves a place in heaven for those who accepts their calling to serve Him.

THE MOON AND STARS

Hebrews 1:10
You, Lord, in the beginning laid the foundation of the earth, and the heavens are the work of your hands.

I come to the garden in the cool of the evening to contemplate all of God's creation.

While there, the moon rises over the eastern horizon, so full and yellow that I gasp in amazement of God's creative hand.

As darkness closes in the stars fill the heavens far and wide, beckoning my soul to join them in their flight.

Free from the tethers of the earth they travel the path set forth by God so long ago.

A guide to sailors upon the open sea, a guide for them to find their way back to their loved ones left behind.

God put a special star in the heavens that night when our Savior was born, a star to bring the wise men to Jesus' side.

A cloud passes just below the moon, like a fleeting ship passing in the night.

The moon lights up the countryside and sparkles across a field of snow when the winter nights are long and cold.

In the spring when thoughts turn to love, the full of the moon quickens the hearts of lovers as they stroll beneath its enchanting light.

God with His mighty hand did all of this to show His love for all of his children who wander the earth in search of peace and tranquility.

Even above the storm clouds, the moon shines bright in the darkest of nights.

When man went to the moon, he found a jewel put there by God for him to contemplate and explore.

Merrill Phillips

From this vantage point man looked back at his blue planet that shined like a sapphire suspended in the darkness of space, a jewel fit for Jesus' crown and gave thanks to the one who put all of this in place.

SEASON OF GIVING

Ephesians 2:8, 10
For by grace you have been saved through faith, and that not of yourselves; it is a gift of God. For we are his workmanship, created in Christ Jesus for good works, which God prepared beforehand that we should walk in them.

Jesus, the Son of God is the greatest gift that man will ever receive.

Jesus came as a babe to live among us and with us, He gives, He gives more than we are ready to receive.

His gifts of love, peace, and comfort are for all of mankind.

Meek and mild He stands by our side, always ready to guide and comfort us when in grief and sorrow we reside.

Never asking anything in return, He gives without demanding or punishing us for being blind.

Jesus came to be a light unto the soul who wants to change and live a life more pleasing unto God on high.

Jesus set us free from the bondage of sin when He gave his life on the cross.

Who else do you know who would die for you without asking for something in return?

No one else would take your sins and mine upon themselves and yet Jesus set us free without expecting something in return.

Jesus did this for you and me when upon that cross He hung, He gave His all so that man through the centuries might have a way to escape the wrath of God.

Draw close unto Jesus and He will draw close unto you and comfort you as through life you go.

As Jesus gives unto you, give unto those you meet on the road of life, for life is precious and a gift from God.

Share that which Jesus has shared with you and your storehouses will never be empty.

Things of the heart are for giving; the more you give the more you will receive.

Don't limit your giving to just one time of year, give all year long and be blessed for being a friend to your fellowman.

THE WRONG DOOR

Luke 12:4-5
And I say to you, my friends, do not be afraid of those who kill the body, and after that have no more that they can do. But I will show you whom you should fear, after He has killed, has power to cast into hell, yes, I say to you, fear Him!

As I lay in bed at night and think of all that I have been through, I thank God for sustaining me.

Jesus died on the cross so that I might be spared the torment of hell.

Hell has a door that swings just one way and once beyond that door there is no other place to go. It is the door to endless torture without reprieve; torment, pain, and the heat of sin are your constant companions.

No water to cool your tongue or fevered brow, just constant cries of anguish is all that will be heard.

There is no shelter from the consequences of the sin that you enjoyed while still here on earth.

Sin might have been sweet in your mouth and perhaps it fulfilled the pleasures of the flesh, but now it is bitter in your belly and you are full of woe.

In hell, there is no "Light" of God to console your soul, in utter darkness you wander through eternity, a lost soul.

Repent my friend before you pass from this life and avoid that door that leads to hell.

Just assuredly, as there is a heaven there is a hell, it was created for all who refuse the love offered by Jesus Christ and from it, there is no return.

Merrill Phillips

There is a great gulf fixed between heaven and hell and no one can pass from one to the other.

It is here and now that we choose to spend eternity in heaven or in hell, choose wisely and regret not your decision to give up the pleasures of sin and follow Jesus Christ all the days of your life.

The pleasures of sin are but for a day, condemnation to hell is for eternity.

THIS AND THAT

Peace shall be unto those who seek the righteousness of God.

* * *

Those who justify themselves are doomed to self-destruction.

* * *

Those who seek God are justified by God.

* * *

The Light of God shines upon all, only the righteous recognize that "Light".

* * *

Peace comes unto those who worship the one who grants that peace, God.

* * *

As the wind drove the sails of old, so does the truths of God drive those who seek Him.

* * *

The fool deceives himself into thinking that God needs his help.

* * *

Once the dawn comes, the dark of night has passed and God's truths still prevail.

*   *   *

Though the body is weak and tired, press on.

*   *   *

Let not the things of this world keep you from following Jesus.

*   *   *

Be wise and choose well what you want to influence your life.

Satan is deceitful and can make wrong seem right and right, wrong.

*   *   *

You will be known by your works, and God knows His own by their heart.

*   *   *

God gives peace to those who toil in His name and admonishes those who stray.

*   *   *

God will respect our decisions in this life and reward us accordingly when before His judgment seat we stand.

*   *   *

God is eager to forgive, so repent and receive His gift of salvation.

* * *

All across the land there are those who are eager to know God, hold not back your knowledge of God.

* * *

Give of yourself freely and seek not personal gain. lest you fall before your fellowman.

* * *

Across the land is a cloud of sin, but through God these clouds can be lifted to allow His Light to shine in our lives.

* * *

God is the same today as in the days of Noah, He never changes.

* * *

It is man who tries to change the image of God to suit himself, thus he knocks on the door to hell.

A receptive heart is called upon to do God's will among his fellowmen, he does it out of joy and love, never thinking of himself.

* * *

A Christian joyfully advances the kingdom of God, always willing to give without receiving.

* * *

It is God's will that a Christian will receive his wages beyond the grave where Satan will never tread.

Merrill Phillips

* * *

The unrighteous are full of trouble and knoweth not where to turn to be cleansed.

* * *

With a smile on his face, man deceives those who cannot see his heart.

* * *

Without truth in his mouth, the heart of man knows many sorrows.

* * *

Man tries night and day to please his loved ones, but without the love of God, he goes astray and betrays those who trust in him.

* * *

Man's eyes are blinded by the treasures of the world and he blocks the treasures of the spiritual realm.

* * *

The clouds of sin block out the Light of God and man falls into the pit of despair.

* * *

To submit to God's commands fills the heart of man with an inner joy and an outward concern for his fellowman.

136

TO THE GLORY OF GOD

John 1:14
And the word became flesh and dwelt among us, and
we beheld His glory, the glory as of the only begotten
of the Father, full of grace and truth.

God planted man in the midst of His creation, on the only
planet in our galaxy that can sustain life, as we know it.

Random chance? No, God created all that we see by speaking
the word, He created something from nothing.

God is a creative God and has more love, compassion and
creativity than all of mankind put together.

His attributes are way beyond our imagination or
comprehension to understand, His mysteries were meant to be
accepted by faith and faith alone.

God has showered us with gifts, gifts that are meant to glorify
Him, not ourselves, we can bring our gifts to fruition or let them
die on the vine.

Those who accept their gifts and cultivate them layup treasures
in heaven, those who reject their gifts will one day regret not having
developed them.

Now is the time to exercise our gifts, water them, and then
share them with our fellowman for the glorification of God here
on earth.

It is folly for man to glorify himself, for all self-glory will come
to not and when man is gone so will his glory be gone.

It is God, not man who created all things; therefore, it is God
who deserves all of the credit and glory, not man, for without God
man can do nothing.

Man was created to serve God, not self or self-interests, God created man and set him free to walk the pathway of life to suit himself.

Some choose to glorify God, while others fall prey to the temptations of the evil one.

As real and satisfying as these temptations may seem they are nothing but means by which Satan can attack God through man.

Satan has the power of temptation only and can by no means force anyone to obey him, he can be very persuasive, but when faced with the truths of God he will flee from us, for he too is submissive to God.

Satan cannot reach beyond the grave, man will spend eternity beyond the grave and whatsoever decisions that man makes before his death will determine where he will spend eternity.

God did not intend for man to be lost, but He will honor whatever decision man makes concerning his eternal destination and will reward man accordingly.

Free choice is a gift from God; an obedient child follows the path of righteousness, whereas a disobedient child follows the way of the flesh.

As long as man puts God first in his life, he will prosper in ways theretofore unknown and will bring glory to God, not himself.

TRUE LOVE PRODUCES FREEDOM

John 3:16
For God so loved the world that He gave His only
begotten Son, that whoever believes in Him should not
perish but have everlasting life.

When you love someone it has to be more than a physical love, you have to love him or her enough to let him or her be themselves.

To hold someone from being himself or herself is selfish and can stifle a person to the point where they are not much more than a slave.

Just as a prisoner can be free, even though they are confined to a prison cell one has to let their mate be free within the bounds of their wedding vows.

We cannot truly love until we are free from bondage by a selfish love.

Jesus demonstrated true love by releasing us to do with our lives as we see fit for ourselves.

By being free, we love and respect our mate because we want to, not because we have to.

The words "have to" put limits on us, it restricts what God intended for us to do and be within the confines of marriage.

To be loved we have to give love away and in so doing love will be returned to us many folds over.

There is a great difference from having to love someone and wanting to love someone, the word "want" implies a choice to love or not to love.

As God set us free out of love, so must we set our mate and friends free out of our love for them. Freedom brings togetherness, restrictions or self-will invites disaster.

It is not enough just to love, love sets us free to develop into the person that God would have us be.

God so loved us that he allowed his Son, Jesus Christ, to be a sacrifice for our sins and so must we love enough to set friends and family free to love God more than they love us.

One who stays in a relationship other than the reason that they want to be there is not free, they are bound by some bondage.

True love is freedom and freedom demonstrates love.

TRUST

Proverbs 3:5
Trust in the Lord with all your heart, and lean not on
your own understanding; in all your ways acknowledge
Him, and He shall direct your paths.

I trust in the Lord my God, in Him I shall not fear.

Though I walk through the valley of sin, He will guide my feet
in the path of righteousness.

His staff shall smite the evil that tries to overwhelm me.

His "Light" shall shine as a beacon of hope, and quiet my fears.

Blessed shall I be if I forsake the flesh and abide in the spirit
until the coming of the Lord.

Though the clouds of sin may overshadow me, God will
provide a safe refuge.

My heart shall not faint when this life I depart, it shall rejoice
as heavenward my spirit climbs.

Mine eyes shall behold the countenance of the God of the
universe and I shall rejoice as He welcomes me home.

Never again to have to live in the shadow of evil or bend to the
whims of evil.

Free to roam the spiritual realm and to eat of the fruit of the
tree of life.

My soul shall sing praises to the Father of us all, and I shall
bend my knees before His throne in submission to His will.

Until the coming of that day, I will love my neighbor as myself
and await the moving of the Spirit that will set me free.

Holy is His name and forgiving is His game, He looses the
bonds of sin and sets my spirit free, trusting in Him all the way
from the cradle to the grave.

TRUST AND OBEY

Proverbs 3:5
Trust in the Lord with all your heart, and lean not unto
your own understanding.

One day I am going to live with my friend Jesus, I am going
to close my eyes in death and make that trip to heaven.

Jesus promised if I lived my life as I should and believe that He
is the Son of God that He would be waiting for me on the other
side of death's door.

Jesus came to earth over two thousand years ago and paid the
price for my sins and yours so that when we die we could live
with Him.

It isn't everyone who would or could do something like that,
Jesus is special and He loves us so much that He gave Himself for
all who believe.

Jesus is the only one who has the power to raise us from the
dead and restore us to perfect health at the final resurrection.

Jesus' love has no bounds, it can heal the sick, it can restore
sight to the blind, it can make the lame walk, and if we ask Him
into our lives, He can save us from the torture of hell.

Jesus has such great love for all that He will forgive us our sins
if we come to Him in humbleness and ask forgiveness from the
depths of our heart.

He has also prepared a new world where there will be no more
sin, a place where there will be no more temptation, a place for all
who acknowledge Him as the Son of God and make Him the Lord
and Master of their lives.

Whom else do you know who would be willing to do all of
these things for you and me?

Satan wouldn't, oh, he will promise us all kinds of things to entice us to follow him, but he doesn't have the power to grant them, nor does he ever intend to give us anything but grief.

Satan is just interested in the destruction of all of God's creation that he can and he will use us for that purpose if we give in to his temptations and in the process, we will become victims of his evil deeds.

As much power that Satan seems to have it is limited to the power of temptation, for he can in no way force anyone to obey him against their will or do his destruction for him without our consent.

If we fall prey to Satan's temptations it is because we do not exercise the truths of God on our own behalf, for Satan will flee when the truths of God are used against him, he is a liar and the father of all lies.

Satan knows that he has but a short time left in his reign of terror here on earth, he knows that he will soon be cast into the lake of fire along with the rest of the fallen angels and he will do as much destruction that he can before this happens.

God gave us the freedom of choice, to either follow Him or to follow Satan and if you choose to follow Satan then we had better be prepared to suffer the same fate as awaits Satan and his fallen angels.

As for me I am going to follow Jesus because I love and respect Him as my personal Savior and as God's one and only Son.

Jesus has what I want and he has granted me eternal life with Him, Satan can only offer the second death (separated from God for eternity).

Through trust and obedience, everyone can be spared the fate of being cast into the lake of fire where the worm never dies and the torment never ceases, this is the choice of each and every one of us, great and small.

TRUST IN THE UNSEEN

Hebrews 11:6
But without faith it is impossible to please Him, for he who comes to God must believe that he is a rewarder of those who diligently seek Him.

Through trust and faith in the unseen things of God, one is able to withstand the onslaught of Satan.

One need not know all the ways of God to survive, just accept them by faith and we shall live beyond the grave.

God has laid out a path for us to follow and if we walk therein, He will bless us all of our days.

Without God and His ever guiding hand we would be like wandering souls in the desert of sin and would die the death of an unrepentant sinner.

Question not the ways of God, follow them all the days of your life and He will not deny you on that great day of judgment.

Accept His will and bend thy knees before his throne and your life will be blessed.

Deny God and He will deny you, leaving you helpless before the onslaught of Satan, facing a future without hope of redemption.

Satan rejoices every time a child of God goes astray; let him not rejoice over you.

God is supreme, He has and always will have the last word as to where one will spend eternity, follow God and live, follow Satan and die the death.

Faith and trust in the unseen does not come easy to those who have turned from God, it takes a desire from within the heart to give one the strength and courage to turn from their evil ways and walk the path of righteousness.

Trust without God is as faith without an understanding of God, trust and faith go hand in hand; one without the other cannot stand.

Trust is likened unto a man who turns from his evil ways and walks the road of faith in the unseen things of God and lives his life for the purpose of promoting God's kingdom here on earth.

UNDER GOD

Luke 1:47
And my spirit has rejoiced in God my Savior.

Almighty God, the one who spoke and the universe leaped into existence.

The ultimate source of all good, the one who points His finger and it is done.

When we follow God we cannot fail, nor can we be easily lead astray.

When tempted we know in our hearts whether it is of God or the evil one.

Knowing God is without a doubt the greatest experience that one can have, all else here on earth is mundane compared to God.

Precious God be with us as we venture forth and spread Your word in a world that is hungry for good news.

Your love as set forth in the Bible is the greatest testimony of Your love for mankind that there is.

All that man needs to know is set forth in the Bible and when put to practice leads to the foot of the cross and eternal life with God.

We who diligently follow you O Lord do so willingly, rather than follow the ways of the flesh.

The ways of the flesh leads to self-destruction either here or hereafter.

With humble hearts, we seek Thee O God, take our hand and lead us where you want us to go.

All doubts and hesitations come from our mortal enemy, Satan.

Your Son, Jesus Christ, defeated Satan while He hung on the cross and gave us the victory, nothing is impossible for us to accomplish through Jesus.

Too many are walking around and know not what life is all about, just taking and giving nothing back or giving credit where credit is due.

Spreading the word is one of the greatest commandments that Jesus gave us.

WAITING PATIENTLY

Isaiah 40:31
But those who wait on the Lord shall renew their strength; they shall mount up with wings like eagles, they shall run and not be weary, they shall walk and not faint.

Wait patiently for the Lord to move, wait for Him to reveal His ways.

Thank the Lord for all of your blessings; praise Him in all that you do.

Wait for His mighty hand to stir the healing waters, wait patiently, even while you rest.

When God's promises are brought to mind, behold, God fulfills His promises, He holds nothing back.

From the rising of the sun to the setting of the moon, He displays His handiwork before our eyes.

Slow to anger, quick to forgive, when we repent He remembers not our iniquities.

His Son, Jesus Christ, died in our stead; He freed us from the hand of the fouler.

Peace reigns where He treads, forgiveness is in His right hand.

With the breath of His mouth, He moves the mighty ships upon the face of the seas.

His love is never ending; He heals the scars of the nations, and brings peace to the repentant soul.

Praise His name while He can yet be found, praise Him and live forever.

Come close to God and He will come close to you, spread His word and wag not thy tongue against Him, for surly the wicked shall not prevail.

Be a carrier of His good news, spread it from sea to sea, and wait patiently for His return and He will reward you abundantly.

Peace is to those who believe and wait upon the Lord, waste not thy time on frivolous things, prepare for what is yet to come, again, wait patiently upon the Lord.

WHERE DOES YOUR
WEALTH LAY

2 Corinthians 8:9
For you know the grace of our Lord Jesus Christ, that
though He was rich; yet for your sakes He became
poor; that you through His poverty might become rich.

We need not have worries of what we shall eat or what we
shall wear or the where withal that we pay our bills, for God will
provide all of our needs.

Earthly wealth was never intended to be hoarded or a means by
which one need not work.

There is nothing in the Bible that says that man should retire
at a given age and never work again, as a matter of fact it states that
man shall labor all of his days.

We are commanded to give of our wealth and distribute it to
the poor and by doing so, we are laying up treasures in heaven.

By helping the poor, they are able to rise above poverty and in
turn reach out and help others less fortunate than themselves.

Wealth has never made anyone happy, nor has it ever kept
anyone from becoming sick or dying.

Money can buy influence and position here on earth, it can
buy the best medical treatment, it can buy all of our wants, but it
cannot buy peace of mind or contentment in our heart.

Too many hoard and make money their god, only to find out
that it is worthless in the kingdom of God.

God should be the center of our lives and He alone should we
worship and through worshipping Him He will supply us with all
of our needs.

As humans, we all would like to have more money, but what would we do with it if we had it?

Would we reach out to those less fortunate than ourselves or would we hoard it. Money can bring a false sense of security.

Would we reach out to other cultures and help supply their needs or would we think them unworthy of our efforts?

With wealth come great responsibilities and the possibility of turning from God and ignoring his commandment of doing unto others as we would have them do to unto us.

Wouldn't you want someone to reach out to you in your times of need, for any one can become destitute at any given time. No one is exempt from needing help, whether it is financial or spiritual.

Wealth comes in many forms, one of these is good health, and one who has good health is among the wealthiest people in the world.

Monetary wealth can bring freedom from want, but it cannot bring freedom from worry or disease, nor can it bring peace of mind, only God can supply these.

All things are gifts from God and are expected to be used to the benefit of all, they are not meant to be hoarded.

We came into this world with nothing and we shall leave this world with nothing, all belongs to God, we are allowed to use what God has for us, but in no way can earthly things get us into heaven.

WITH EVERY TRIAL

1Peter 4:12-13
Beloved, do not think it strange concerning the fiery trial which is to try you, as though some strange thing happened to you; but rejoice to the extent that you partake of Christ's sufferings, that when His glory is revealed, you also may be glad with exceeding joy.

With every trial that we endure, a little more dross is removed from our lives and we become a little more like Jesus.

All trials and tribulations are basically designed for us to grow closer to God and to become more dependent upon Him to see us through this life in a successful manner.

It is not hard to see that many refuse to allow God to have a positive effect on their lives and that they depend upon themselves to supply their needs.

This type of relationship can and does lead to a meaningless life, especially when we come to the end of our lives and have no idea of where we will spend eternity.

God being God allows us to live our lives as we see fit for ourselves, however He is there waiting for us to come to Him on our own and ask for His guidance in our lives.

Those who do turn to God in their times of need find that He will guide them and comfort them in whatever trial that they may be facing, and will supply an answer.

It is with pleasure that God bestows upon His children the comfort and answers that they need in their daily lives; He holds back nothing from those who love Him.

As painful as trials and tribulations may be God will take the sting out of them and provide answers beyond our expectations.

God has the answers to all of our problems, but unfortunately, we often think that we know more about our problems and the best way to solve them than God does, at that point, we ignore God and end up worse than we were before.

Every trial that a Christian goes through enhances their relationship with God and what was meant to be a tool of Satan to drive a wedge between God and a Christian can serve to bring a Christian closer to God.

In all negative situations, there can be good come out of them, for God is in complete control over everything and all situations that we find ourselves in.

God has and always will triumph over evil, for He is the ultimate source of all power and in no wise can He be over ruled or removed from any situation, even though we may try to remove Him.

One of the promises of God is that He will be with us when we face the trials of life, and if we allow Him, He will not only guide us, He will make our paths straight.

LIST OF BOOKS
BY MERRILL PHILLIPS

MY CALLING
TELL ME AGAIN GRAMPA
PRICE OF FREEDOM
THOUGHTS FOR THE SOUL
LIVING BY HIS WORD
POTOURRI
FOOD FOR THOUGHT
WALKING THE PATHWAY OF LIFE
LIGHTING THE WAY
WHERE THE SAND MEETS THE SEA

At the age of eighty-seven the author still enjoys
putting pen to paper, encouraging others to
turn to the Scriptures to find solutions to
the problems of life. He also encourages
others to become followers of Jesus
Christ and receive the gift of
eternal life that He offers
to those who believe
in Him.